The
Romance AND Adventures OF ROGER KING M.D.

Byron B. Oberst M.D., FAAP

Order this book online at www.trafford.com
or email orders@trafford.com

Most Trafford titles are also available at major online book retailers.

Print information available on the last page.

ISBN: 978-1-4907-6077-3 (sc)
ISBN: 978-1-4907-6076-6 (e)

Trafford rev. 06/23/2015

www.trafford.com
North America & international
toll-free: 1 888 232 4444 (USA & Canada)
fax: 812 355 4082

CONTENTS

Part 4
Life at Fort Dix and Brown's Mills

Part 5
Destination Yokohama
Captain Roger King M.D. USAC

Part 6
Sendai, Japan
The 172nd Station Hospital

Part 7
On the High Seas Again

Part 8
Back Home at Last

Detroit, Michigan

OVERVIEW

The Romance and Adventures of Roger King M.D.

Part 1
Roger King M.D. – Intern
The Life of a Neophyte Physician

Part 2
Roger King M.D. – Resident
The Molding of a Pediatrician

Part 3
Roger King M.D. – US Army Medical Corps
Lieutenant Roger King M.D. USMC

Part 4
Life at Fort Dix and Brown's Mills

Part 5
Destination Yokohama
Captain Roger King USMC

Part 6
Sendai, Japan
172nd Station Hospital

Part 7
On the High Seas Again
Stateside Bound

Part 8
Back Home at Last
Detroit and the Henry Ford Hospital

Epilogue

DEDICATION

To the memory of my Wonderful
Beloved Mary Catherine
She was my anchor and the light of my life for 66 years
To my Three Sons, Who taught me so much.
Byron
Terrance
Matthew

Mary at Age 20

Mary and Obie in the Early Years

Mary and Obie at Age 68

BOOKS BY B.B. OBERST M.D., FAAP

Practical Guidance for Pediatric and Adolescent Practice

Computer Applications to Private Practice – A Primer

Co-Editor: R. Reid M.D.

Computers in Private Practice Management

Co-Editor: J. Long PhD

Reflections on Pediatric Medicine from 1943 to 2010

    A Dual Love Story

A Mother, Her Three Sons, and Their Dog

    The Love Story of a Father for His Family

Miracles and Other Unusual Medical Experiences

The Golden Years: Living in a Retirement Center

Acknowledgements

To my Beloved Mary, who always inspired me to strive to do my best and comforted me when I was low in spirits

To my wonderful sons, who married very special wives.

To my major Editor, Terrance, who drove me crazy with his innumerable corrections and caustic comments.

To my lovely Daughter-in-law, Shirley, whose comments helped to improve this work

To my many friends who have made my life worthwhile living here at The Immanuel Lakeside Village – they are the inspiration for this current book.

PROLOGUE

It was in the year 1943 that the medical students had to endure a very grueling educational pathway. At their very first lecture in Embryology, Dr. Latta, the Professor of this Department, said to Roger's class of one hundred and eight, "Look at the person on either side of you, one of you will not be here to graduate!" Help! "Please do not let it be me," thought Roger" as he looked around the room and saw PHD's, Pharmacists, Business Men, Teachers, and many others. He learned that he was the second youngest person in his class. There was only one woman in this entire group. How was he going to compete with this entourage of talent?

During the first two years of Roger's academic sojourn, he studied what each of the body organs were and how they functioned together within the whole body. Anatomy was the foundation for his understanding of the various aspects of the organs, their relationships, and how they were joined together into a functioning entity. Roger loved studying what makes us human beings tick and ended up being one among the top ten students in this particular subject.

During his second year, he learned how the body physiologically functioned and how the various organ systems were interrelated and the different chemical reactions were carried out within this anatomic structure. The fields of Physiology and Biochemistry were the keystones of that year's academic progress. He so enjoyed the study of Physiology. Roger King studied hard during these preliminary years. Because of the compressed pre-med curriculum due to the coming war, he only time for the required four hours of biochemistry instead of the recommended eight. He suffered accordingly in the related subjects of Biochemistry and Pharmacology.

His next two years were clinical ones and were devoted to applying all of this accumulated knowledge to the practical study of the different medical impacts disease had upon this marvelous creation – the body.

At the conclusion of these grinding years, he had to be tutored in the practical applications of all of this knowhow. The initial part of this preceptorship was the internship with its general exposure to all of the different fields of medicine; thence, after weighing his own medical interests and bents, he entered into his residency years to concentrate his endeavors and studies in a particular discipline of the vast regions of medicine. He had an inkling that Pediatrics was going to be the field of his life's endeavors.

At the conclusions of all of this training, he had to take a series of tests to ascertain or not that he was qualified to go forth and treat members of society.

His roadway had been a long and arduous journey from highschool onward, but doctors had to be individually hand crafted and could **Not** be mass produced. Sad but true; some of the smartest students made the poorest physicians as they had no insight into what constitutes a real live human being [bedside manner]. They were great with a textbook or a test tube, but failed miserably when confronted, at the bedside of a real live person. Their bedside manner was non-existent. Any resemblance of this manner was purely coincidental and sadly lacking within their personalities.

Dr. Latta's prediction had come true. There were only eighty-six classmates left to graduate. This education had been a real grind filled with many hardships and headaches. It felt great that it was behind him.

PART 1

ROGER KING M.D.

THE MAKING OF A NEOPHYTE PHYSICIAN

CHAPTER 1

GRADUATION AND ITS AFTERMATH

The story begins on a cold blustery March day in 1946. The winds swirled around chasing dust motes here and there. The somber, sullen, leaded, heavy hanging, overcast clouds threatened snow. Already, there were a few flurries gently floating down on hidden air currents only to disintegrate into nothing when alighting on the ground.

Groups of people were hurrying into the Civic Auditorium to escape the chilling winds. Excitement was in the air, and families were in eager anticipation for the ceremonies to start. This day was the end of a long six year grind by the graduates where they had had to cope with the compression of the entire four years of the intense study of medicine into just three years due to World War II. As an antecedent, they had had to squeeze the minimum three years of pre-med work into two and a half years in order to enter into med school in March instead of the usual fall academic starting; the Armed Services needed to ensure a continuing supply of physicians. This grind was a real drudge, drag, and back breaker. It was no easy task for the weak of heart.

At last, the auditorium lights dimmed, the audience hushed, and the orchestra started playing that age old "Pomp and Circumstance March" indicative of a graduation ceremony. The eager medical degree candidates, in their black robes, began their solemn, slow march to their assigned seats. The faculty was on the stage in their respective impressive and resplendent doctorate robes. This day was a very solemn occasion for the graduates and their families. The innumerable speakers were introduced and droned on saying many words about nothing as the candidates impatiently awaited the receiving their hard earned diplomas. There were eighty-five men and one woman in this class. Few women went into medicine in those days. Dr. Latta's prediction of a twenty-five percent student loss had come to fruition.

Each candidate marched across the stage to receive his cherished diploma, stopped, faced the audience, and changed the tassel on the hat from one side to another depicting that they had completed their degree and now could be considered a "Doctor of Medicine".

The class stood, as a whole, and recited in solemn tones the Hippocratic Oath[1] which would be their mantra forever more. Thus it was spoken:

> *I swear by Apollo the physician, and Aesculapius the surgeon, likewise Hygeia and Panacea, and call all the gods and goddesses to witness, that I will keep this underwritten oath, to the utmost of my power and judgment.*

---
[1] Hippocratic Oath Wikipedia

3

I will reverence my master who taught me the art. Equally with my parents, I will allow him things necessary for his support, will consider his sons as brothers. I will teach them my art without reward or agreement, and I will impart all my acquirements, instructions, and whatever I know, to my master's children, as to my own, and likewise to all my pupils, who shall bind and tie themselves by a professional oath, but to none else.

With regard to healing the sick, I will devise and order them the best diet, according to my judgment and means; I will take care that they suffer no hurt or damage.

Nor shall any man's entreaty prevail to administer poison to anyone; neither will I counsel any man to do so. Moreover, I will get no sort of medicine to any pregnant woman, with a view to destroy the child.

Further, I will comport myself and use my knowledge In a godly manner.

I will not cut for the stone, but will commit that affair entirely to the surgeons.

Whatsoever house I may enter, my visit shall be for the convenience and advantage of the patient; and I willingly refrain from doing any injury or wrong from falsehood, and [in a special manner] from acts of an amorous nature, whatever may be the rank of those who it may be my duty to cure, whether mistress or servant, bond or free.

Whatever, in the course of my practice, I may see or hear [even when not invited], whatever I may happen to obtain knowledge of, if it not be proper to repeat it, I will keep sacred and secret within my own breast.

If I faithfully observe this oath, may I thrive and prosper in my fortune and profession, and live in the estimation of posterity, or on breach thereof, may the reverse be my fate.

This oath was given with great solemnity and grave feelings. As Roger recited these words out loud, his mind reverted to thoughts of all those great physicians who had gone before him and took this same oath, and blazed their way through new medical frontiers. It was a very telling moment for him. Roger was about to enter into that great healing profession, and his inherent inadequacy made itself felt down to his toes. He wondered whether or not he could measure up to the grave responsibilities he would soon face.

At long last, the ceremony was concluded; and the celebrants would begin joyful parties with their families and close friends. There was a pleasant sensation awaiting the folks as they filed from the auditorium. The skies had cleared and seemed to want to add to the joy of this momentous occasion. The clouds had blown away, and in their place was sunshine and happiness as though the weather wanted to join in the joy with the happy people.

The only fly in this great accomplishment had been the need for Roger to pass the "State Board of Medical Examiners Test" before he could become an intern. He must be a licensed physician in order to become a qualified intern and practicing doctor.

When he returned home, before the family festivities began and the invited guests began to arrive, the mail was resting quietly in the curbside mailbox. With great trepidation, he sorted through the mail. There it was! His internship acceptance or rejection letter resided within his hand. Dare he open it and find out his fate? He so wanted to intern at the Omaha Medical Center and Teaching Hospital. It was a plum to be chosen to work there. As it was a state institution, a means test [meaning that patients had to meet a financial ceiling] was necessary to be treated at this facility; hence, the greater the freedom and the assumption of much more responsibility the interns had as contrasted with an internship in a private hospital.

The advantages of a rotating internship in a teaching hospital were multifold by gaining experience in the many different fields of medicine. The basic premise of these types of hospital was to prepare neophyte physicians concerning the different requirements needed for a general medical practice or to assist them in deciding what medical specialty they might desire to enter.

With knots in his stomach and with sweaty hands, he shakily opened this envelop. His face broke out with a grin from ear to ear, and his face beamed with delight when he found that he was one of eight fellows favored for this great opportunity at the med center. Once again, he vowed to himself that he would endeavor to become a worthy doctor and to be a credit to his chosen profession. He could hardly wait to tell his family.

His internship would start on April 1 and would last for fifteen months pending the outcome of his State Board Examination. Interning in a teaching hospital was such a desired position; and would present many great learning experiences for him as contrasted with being an intern in a private hospital facility. There would be many more hands-on opportunities for care and decision making available. Because of World War II needs, the previous classes finished their four years of schooling; and, then, had to endure only a nine month internship as the Army quickly needed the doctors.

The medical schools all over the country desired to return to the four year curriculum, now that the War had ended, and the twelve month internship was reinstituted; thus, his class was chosen to bridge this three month gap and donate the time of fifteen months for the cause célèbre. As most of the physicians were in the service there were no resident available to help teach interns, thus, these eight, were all there were. God Help them in this awesome job! As most of the volunteer clinical faculty were swamped with their own patients due to the scarcity of physicians, their personal supervision was going to be severely curtailed. They would be on their own much of the time!

Roger was to report to the hospital April 1, 1946. Before hand, he was to obtain several white intern outfits with the high button neck collars and was to wear clean white rubber soled shoes at all times while in the hospital. Meanwhile, he endured taking the mind wearying and mind boggling State Board Medical examination. The testing lasted over three hours of grueling and fatiguing questions on everything imaginable in medicine.

While picking out his outfits, he felt so important. His last need in this sequence of events reached its finality when the mail delivered to him the notice of his passing the State Boards. This epistle included his Medical License Certificate and Number allowing him to practice medicine. The license must be displayed in a prominent situation wherever he worked; his assigned license number was 8448. Wow! What a thrill this letter was! He had to immediately notify his parents and close friends. He felt so proud and was more than ready to go forth to "Save Lives and to Stamp out Disease". Ha!

Finally, the fateful day came. He reported to the office of the Omaha Medical Center and Teaching Hospital's Administrator, Alan Moser. Many instructions were given to him concerning hospital rules and regulations. Subsequently, Roger was assigned a small room in the intern living area, which would literally be his home for next fifteen month; given a mailbox; and was told that his stipend would be $25 dollars per month with room, board, and laundry included.

His first rotation would start with pediatrics. He had requested this service as he wanted to determine early on if this area was to be his chosen field. He hoped that this would be his vocation for a lifetime of work.

He was presented with the Hospital's Intern Manuel which would be his bible for the ensuing months. It listed several essential facts some of which were:

1. He would make his Ward Rounds on his assigned patients starting at 8:00 am each and every morning regardless of when he finally retired to bed.
2. Any new admission to his assigned ward **MUST** have the patient's history, physical examination, and required lab work by the examiner per Se accomplished by eight am regardless of what time the admission occurred. There were no after hour laboratory technicians available. He had to personally do the blood counts, urine tests, and take any necessary X-rays at the time of the admission.
3. No females were allowed in the Intern Quarters
4. There would be no smoking or drinking in the Quarters.
5. Meals would be eaten in the Hospital Cafeteria
6. Laundry would be placed outside one's door every Monday morning.

There were many, many others too numerous to be listed here. With all of these rules and regulations, he began to wonder what kind of life this was going to be. It seemed as though his heart and soul would not be his own for the next fifteen months; and so it came to pass.

CHAPTER 2

ROGER'S INITIAL SERVICE - PEDIATRICS

On the third day of Roger's pediatric service, the hospital paging system sang out loud and clear, "Dr. King report to the Emergency Room immediately"! As he hurried to this area, his mind was a jumble of thoughts. "What all could this call be concerning?" Upon his arrival, Tom Viner, who was the intern assigned to the ER, led him into an examining room. There on the table was a small waif of a child of about fifteen months of age. He was filthy from head to toe and even had some feces smeared on his body.

Roger was told, "There are no parents with this child, "Jimmy". His aging Aunt is raising him and is not too reliable for this task; therefore, the Child Protective Services brought him to the Emergency Room because of apparent child abuse, so what you see is what you get, "How sad for the child".

Roger could not agree more and turned with a bewildered mind to the patient, wondering to himself, "How to handle this child without any history to begin with?" He had never been exposed to this type of situation before. Roger proceeded to examine this child.

During the physical examination, Roger noted that the child could not open his mouth when he was trying to examine it and his throat with a tongue blade. If the examining table was jarred, the child went into severe muscle spasms. The patient's abdomen was as rigid as a board; the child had a strange and peculiar grimace to his face with a fixed smile and raised eye brows. Could these facial features be what was described in the textbooks as "Risus Sardonicus?"

Thoughts began to tumble into some sort of sequence in Roger's mind. "Could this possibly be a case of Tetanus" [Lockjaw], he recalled that he had written his senior thesis on Tetanus and the new Tetanus Toxoid which had been developed to protect our wounded soldiers from this devastating disorder after receiving a battlefield wound. This knowledge came to mind because in those days, medical schools required from their graduating students, similar to any doctorate degree student, a typed and bound thesis on some research subject before graduation could occur. Many years later, this requirement was abandoned in the early 1960's. This thesis went into the medical library as a reference book.

Roger, remembering those findings as a junior medical student, Jimmy seemed to fit the tetanus criteria of Lockjaw. He had been assigned a case regarding a forty year old mother of four, who had fallen in her barnyard and sustained a compound fracture of her ankle with the bone protruding out through the skin. Her spouse and all the farm workers were out in the fields harvesting; so there was no one to assist her. With sheer grit, she managed to drag herself through the barnyard to her house in order to phone for help. The tetanus spores could live in the ground for as much as twenty years and still cause trouble. The tetanus bacteria lived naturally in the horse's intestinal tract. Wherever there was horse manure, there was the threat of tetanus. She later died from this horrible lockjaw situation as there was very little that could be done in those early days. It was a horrible death and left a huge impression on Roger.

The tetanus bacteria needed to thrive in a low oxygen state; thus, puncture wounds and similar wounds were ideal places for tetanus spores to harbor and cause great harm by the poisonous toxin they produced. There was no effective antibiotic available in those early days. Roger had been a junior medical student when he saw the first shot of Penicillin given at the med center. Tetanus was NOT affected by Penicillin.

Roger decided then and there to call Dr. Gedgoud, the Professor of Pediatrics, who was one of the two full time faculty members in house. The rest of the teaching faculty were all Volunteers; hence the greater responsibility the interns had to assume.

Dr. Gedgoud ran the pediatric department, was salaried by Maternal and Child Health fees – not by the University. He was a splendid diagnostician of sick children along with being a superb teacher. He came, examined the child, and concurred with Roger's tentative diagnosis; then, the party began in earnest.

In those days, there were no private rooms on the wards except for one in which to isolate contagious diseases. The beds were separated from each other by means of drapes that could be pulled around for a bit of privacy. There were twenty beds and eight cubicles in the ward to handle the pediatric patients. The nurses' station was just adjacent to the cubicles and rendered a clear view of the ward beds.

The child was admitted to a pediatric cubicle where a feeding tube was slipped into his stomach via his nose as he couldn't open his mouth to drink fluids, eat, or chew. A special nutritious formula was given to him four times a day via the tube. Dr. Gedgoud explained in detail to Roger the next step in this child's care. He would have to check the rigidity of the abdomen and determine the amount of liquid "Avertin" [a mild relaxing sedative which was eliminated from the body through the lungs by the expelled air while breathing] to be given rectally. There was a sweet pungent odor to the expelled air. Ugh!

The amount of "Avertin" given was based upon a patient's weight per a chart indicating the dosage recommended. This procedure was to relax the abdominal muscles as this intense rigidity drained the body resources and could cause a demise by itself through mere patient exhaustion. The dosage must be exact or dire consequences could occur. No nurse was allowed to handle this chore. This job required Roger's undivided attention if this child had a chance to survive at all.

A large injection of Tetanus antitoxin was given to neutralize the bacteria's toxic antibodies, which were circulating in the blood stream, and causing this rigidity problem. This toxin was classified as a neurotoxin as it affected many nerves throughout the body.

Close overall examination of the child failed to reveal a portal of entry for the bacteria which caused the tetanus and/or other physical problems. How did the tetanus invade this body remained a mystery. It loved to live deep in body tissues where there was very little oxygen as it was classified as an anaerobic bacteria, and usually occurred with puncture type wounds.

For the next ten days, Roger had to get up every three hours night and day, check the abdominal rigidity, and determine what dose of "Avertin" was necessary to be administered. The nurses would call him about five minutes before the dose was due. Talk about fatigue! He would stumble down to the ward rousing himself while on his way. Never had he been so tired. It seemed as though, just as he would be getting to sleep, it would be time to answer the nurse's call to check the patient. After awhile, the process of getting back to sleep became simple and lasted throughout the remainder of his internship days.

There was a doorbell high on the wall in his room. When a call came for him, the resulting sound could awaken the dead! He had to walk down the hall to the phone as there was no such luxury of having one in each room. By the time he would arrive at the phone, he would be wide awake and ready for whatever awaited him on the other end of the line.

Roger became fond of the quietness of the hospital when going to the ward to answer a call. There was a peacefulness which permeated the hospital halls as he hurried along. As he walked towards his destination, the only sounds he would hear were those of his rubber soled shoes squeaking on the hall floor covering. There was a certain restfulness created in his mind while he strolled along.

He would hustle down the hallway shaking his head to clear out the cobwebs. Because of this shrill noise happened every three hours while asleep, Roger developed a very responsive "Startle Reflex", which lasted most of his lifetime; thereafter, even into his subsequent retirement years. It was such a nuisance and a major irritant to be aroused by a phone's shrill ringing by Roger almost jumping out of bed. This reflex lasted for so many years.

Roger would take a very cold shower to rouse himself each morning before beginning his ward rounds. He needed to be sure that his mind was bright and alert before meeting with Dr. G. When he would first look at himself in the mirror, Oh My Lord! He viewed a bleary, red eyed face topped with an unkempt mop of chestnut brown hair. Ugh! What looked back at him was an appearance that only a mother could love, and even she might have some difficulty..

He would trudge down to the third floor pediatric ward, test the child's abdominal muscles, and based upon his subjective evaluation of the muscle state, the necessary amount of "Avertin" would be measured and instilled into the child's rectum very slowly through a rubber tube so that medicine could be absorbed in its entirety; then, hopefully, Roger would go back to bed for a few hours of blessed sleep until the next call came. He, also, learned to exist while harboring a chronic fatigue state of mind and body. This continuum of events went on and on for ten days at least.

At long last, the abdominal rigidity gradually lessened; and the child began to slowly recover. When the child was ready for discharge, the hospital Social Service Department took over this case and contacted the Child Protective Services to determine if it was suitable for him to return home or not, based upon what the extenuating circumstances had been prior to his admission..

Everyone on the ward took great delight in this child's survival. All the ward personnel were very proud of his recovery and took pride in their contributions and accomplishments. This boy had become everyone's pet. Survival with this disease was a very rare feat in those days. Roger felt that he had passed his first big practical pediatric examination successfully. Later on, he often wondered what had become of Jimmy; but he was never to learn. Wow! He was a happy intern in this accomplishment. His colleagues and the nursing staff began to have respect for Roger's diligence and clear headed thinking.

Every Monday morning was "Urine Day". Ugh! There was a small, equipped laboratory adjacent to the pediatric ward where Roger had to perform a urinalysis on each specimen collected from every ward patient. This testing was considered a nuisance type of job and was accomplished with very little self satisfaction.

The task included testing for sugar, protein, color of the urine, and specific gravity, and with a microscopic study for white cells and/or red blood cells. If the child was a diabetic, an additional quantitative sugar determination had to be done. It was imperative that the results be entered onto the child's medical chart before 8:00 am; consequently, Roger started his Mondays extra early..

At precisely 8:00 am, Dr. Gedgoud would arrive on the ward dressed in his long white laboratory coat for morning rounds on the patients. If Roger was working in the laboratory, out of the corner of his eye, he could see a white coat go sailing by the door. This event notified Roger to stop whatever he was doing, and that it was time to begin the formal ward rounds with the boss man. There were usually, at least, twenty children and/or infants housed on the ward at all times.

The pediatric rounds were the highlight of the day for Roger. Each child's chart notes was religiously studied for progress from the previous day, and all of the student nursing notes were read verbatim in their entirety. If there was any questionable data, the involved nursing student was called upon to come to the ward and explain her notes. Too bad, if she was asleep from working the night shift before; she came anyway.

Roger learned the importance that the nurses' notes contained a plethora of information regarding a patient's condition, food offered and what was eaten. The child's intake and output of fluids was religiously and carefully recorded as it was vital that the child be kept well hydrated. Roger learned that fluid balance was a critical item to observe on any child/adult for whatever reason the patient was being treated. Daily weights were written down. Roger, quickly, learned that the nurses were the eyes and ears, regarding each patient old and young, for the doctor; thus it was necessary to study the patient's chart carefully; and, to make any necessary changes in the child's care protocol. These important and primary lessons were engraved in and on Roger's mind and heart for evermore. This chart study molded Roger's patient rounds all the way through his future care of patients when out in practice years.

After the all charts were studied, each child was seen and examined physically for any changes from the day before. Dr. Gedgoud loved to play a game with his interns. If Roger asked a question concerning a patient, immediately, Doctor G would ask a question right back to make Roger think and come to some conclusion; then, Dr. G would ask another question of Roger. This repartee would continue until Roger arrived at the correct answer which was the one desired by Dr. G. Roger so enjoyed this morning exercise as it made him think things through to a final conclusion; and, thus, greatly increased his capacity to handle intricate situations on his own both now and into the future.

Roger, himself, used this same Socratic teaching technique later on when he was out in practice and teaching interns and residents. Roger would make his own "Patient Chart Rounds" before Dr. G would arrive; so that he would be prepared for Dr. G's onslaught of questions. It was enjoyable to play this game and, oh! how much he learned at foot of this master teacher.

After the pediatric ward rounds were over, a trip to the newborn nursery was made where the reading of charts and the examination of each infant was accomplished once again. Each infant's weight was carefully studied to be sure of whatever weight gain or loss had taken place. Temperatures were essential to be noted for any elevations or lowered temperatures and were studied with great care. An infant's temperature was a good indicator of the infant's wellbeing

There was an odd tank-like unit in the nursery with an opening in the top for reaching the infant. Dr. G explained that this piece of equipment was a "Hess Bed". It was one of the first modern day and useful incubators for premature infants in order to keep the tiny infant's temperatures stable. Chilling was devastating to any infant and nearly fatal to a premature.

While making rounds one morning, it was noted that one infant had a temperature, seemed somewhat listless, and on examination nothing definite could be determined. Running the causes through Roger's mind, he ventured to mention to Dr. G that the infant might have a sepsis [blood stream infection]. It was imperative to obtain an immediate blood culture. He had never obtained one on a child so small, but he had observed the technique.

The nurse placed the infant in a wrapped mummy blanket so no movement could occur; then, she shaved the infant's head over the anterior fontanel [soft spot] and painted it with "Merthiolate"[an antiseptic solution]. Roger positioned himself at the head of the treatment table; the infant's head was tilted backward over the edge. The nurse held the head very steady.

Roger put on a sterile gown and donned sterile gloves. His index finger probed for the "V" indentation where the two frontal skull bones adjoined each other. With nervous sweat running down his back and his heart pounding, he received the twenty gauge needle and syringe into his hand; and proceeded to insert the needle through the "V" indentation on into the infant's Saggital Sinus venous reservoir, which was located just below the soft spot. He withdrew five cc's of blood; then, he gently withdrew the needle and syringe while simultaneously applying pressure to the needle hole. The blood would endeavor to clotted almost immediately.

The infant's blood was shaken to keep liquid and slowly inoculated into several different types of culture media test tubes. The slowness was necessary so there would be no destruction of the red blood cells [Hemolysis]. The different broths were conducive for different bacteria to grow and to provide enough colony cultures so identification could occur. Once the bacteria was identified appropriate treatment could begin; and would be needed to last for the next ten to twelve days. Meanwhile, the infant was kept in strict isolation. Whew, Roger breathed a deep sigh of relief now that this procedure was successfully accomplished. He felt very good about himself, and his confidence gauge rose several degrees. He began to feel like a real true doctor.

One early morning about 2:00 am, Roger received a call via the demoniac door bell. He staggered to the hall phone where a nurse explained that there was an infant in the nursery crying endlessly and seemingly in pain without any apparent cause. Nothing she did would comfort this infant. By the time Roger arrived at the nursery, he was wide awake and reviewing in his mind some of the more possible reasons for this situation. He very carefully examined the squalling infant, who was seemingly crying nonstop at top of his voice. Roger looked and looked again and couldn't find a smidgen of a reason for the infant's distress. With great reluctance, he decided to call Dr. G at 2:30 am.

A low pitched and sleep filled voice answered the phone, "Hello". Roger explained the infant's situation, and his inability to find anything wrong with the baby. There was a very long and significant pause during which Roger felt his heart sink down to his toes. The sleep filled voice merely said, "Doctor, did you think about feeding the infant?" Bang went the phone, and a dial tone was all that Roger heard. "Oh! Oh!", Roger thought, "I am in the soup now. My days will be numbered in pediatrics if I don't do better than this". Naturally, to rub more salt into Roger's wound when the infant was given a feeding, the infant quieted down and immediately went to sleep. Oh well! Such are the mistakes of a neophyte physician.

Roger enjoyed the peaceful quiet of the night while walking the hospital halls when everyone was asleep; he would muse to himself about the great medical names who had made major contributions in the far past without any known guideposts to point the way. There was Harvey, who discovered the blood circulation; Lister, who promoted sterile techniques before surgery or before delivering babies; Semmelweis, concerning child bed fever, Sir William Osler, the great English diagnostician, and many, many others. Roger's mind was kept busy remembering the antecedent heroes of medicine.

One day, there came an admission from the admitting room of a little five year old black boy, who had gone to visit his Grandma, who lived next door. Willy saw a coke bottle sitting on the table partially filled with a liquid. Oh! how he loved coca cola; so, naturally, he drank the contents. The only sticker in this scenario was the fact that it was not coke in the bottle, but the solution was a lye cleaning material. Oh! Oh!

Grandma was beside herself when she brought Willy to the hospital. It was impossible to console her. She had a great guilt complex. Poor Willy couldn't even swallow water. What to do! Oh what to do! Roger was placed in the middle of an immense quandary. Willy would need to be fed, but the oral route was not feasible. Naturally, Roger consulted Dr. G, and a surgeon was asked to place a tube into the stomach through the abdominal wall in order to bypass the oral passages. This was done Pronto!

A nutritious mixture was given to Willy q.o.d [four times a day]. He maintained his weight and fluid balance on this regimen. The next step in his care was to endeavor to pass a string down through the esophagus into the stomach by Willy endeavoring to swallow it. This solution was doomed to failure right from the get go; it was determined that this route was impossible to achieve.

This situation had everyone's head being scratched for a solution. At last, consultation with the ENT and the Urology Departments made this suggestion, "Dr. Lovgren would endeavor to pass an esophagoscope down towards the stomach and attempt to dilate this organ. In a similar manner, Dr. Lee, a Urologist, would endeavor to pass a cystoscope upward from the stomach via the hole in the stomach which was made for the feeding tube". They would try to slowly dilate the passageway open in this manner at weekly intervals.

This approach was instituted every Saturday morning. For sedation, Willy was given a capsule of "Seconal", [a mild sedative] rectally. The "Seconal" worked like a charm. Willy was very cooperative with this approach. This medication had no after effects on him as It was metabolized very quickly by the body. Each Saturday came and went with some slight progress. After almost a year, the two instruments met and a string was passed. Hurrah!

Now, weekly dilatations could be accomplished by drawing a soft bogie along the string performing the important dilation; thus, it came to pass. After a long period of time with repeated Saturday dilations, Willy was able to swallow on his own and was discharged to return monthly for this procedure; at the last report heard by Roger, Willy was in his fifties and was still being periodically dilated. Roger had long since gone into the field of pediatrics. He had moved onward in his training including a stint in army life.

Roger was sitting at the nurses' station one evening making his nightly rounds. An eight year old boy had had an attack of acute appendicitis that morning which needed immediate surgery as it was close to rupturing. This procedure had been accomplished without any aftermath.

While Roger was at the desk, he casually glanced upward and cast his eyes towards the ward beds. Heaven help us! There was Jack, the immediate post-op patient, hanging and swinging by his knees from the back of his bed. He was giggling and laughing like a loon and really enjoying himself. Roger jumped up with a bound, quickly proceeded to Jimmy's bed, and scolded him in no uncertain terms. A sheepish Jimmy lay back down on his bed, promising that he would not do anymore silly stunts. Roger had an immediate and on the spot lesson in how resilient some children were.

Dickie B. was a five year old child with a kidney problem called. "Nephrosis". His body lost tremendous amounts of protein through his urine output. As a result, his body could not retain water in his blood stream. The fluids would seep out and accumulate in his abdomen causing great distention. At times, he could have trouble breathing as the abdominal distention would interfere with his diaphragm's movement; thus, some fluid had to be removed. This need occurred periodically.

Dr. G explained the procedure to be used to Roger and left him alone to perform it. Roger was petrified. A trochar [great sized needle], was needed to be inserted through the abdominal wall, and the fluid drained off. An injection of Novocain was placed just two inches to the left and two inches below Dickie's navel. Roger, donned sterile gloves and gown, again with great fear and trepidation, he inserted the trochar in slanting upward manner; so that when the trochar was withdrawn, the opening would self seal like a flap due to the intra abdominal pressure.

Once again, Roger performed flawlessly, and the procedure was a great success with no problems occurring to Dickie. Over time, he performed this task several times.

At long last, Roger's six weeks on the pediatric service was completed. He had learned so much under Dr. Gedgoud's tutelage and had formed several good habits for his lifetime in medicine. In addition, he became very adapt in performing several different and important medical procedures. With great reluctance, he moved on to the Men's Ward and Mrs. Mason, the head nurse. She was a known to be a stickler by the interns by demanding exactness and preciseness in any medical orders. Woe to the intern who was not in compliance with her desires.

CHAPTER 3

ON THE MEN'S WARD

Roger walked onto the men's ward at precisely 8:00 am. After his tutoring by Dr. G, he did not entertain any fears or trepidations, he regarded this assignment as another milestone in his medical maturation process.

As he had learned the importance of the daily chart rounds and had this approach ingrained in him by Dr. G., he surprised the head nurse. Mrs. Mason [Mother Mason to the interns], insisted on medical protocol. She expected and demanded that any student nurse working at the chart desk, stand, and greet the doctor on his arrival on the ward. [Unfortunately, those time honored customs and respect for the field of medicine fell by the wayside with the passage of the years]

Mrs. Mason learned and began to respect Roger for his paying close attention to the details put into the nurses' notes. After meticulously studying the different patients' chart, he examined the patients. Mrs. Mason noticed how dedicated and careful he was. She admired those traits.

Mother Mason loved to teach the interns about the need for writing clear and concise orders in the charts. Roger examined Mr. Jones because he coughed so much at night disturbing the other ward patients. He decided that Mr. Jones had a marked sinus infection with a copious postnasal drip which was the culprit causing the night coughing. Accordingly, Roger blissfully wrote, "Hot Packs QID" [four times per day] and went on his merry way with his duties.

Roger, certainly did not miss the Monday morning urinalysis routine of the pediatric ward. All medications ordered had to be found in the hospital pharmacopeia which listing was at each nurse's station. The hospital pharmacy committee decided which medication would be contained in the pharmacy. Any medication ordered could not be ordered if it wasn't listed there. The pharmacist would be required to supply an alternative from the listing. This approach saved considerable money in the stocking of similar medications and eliminated any outlandish orders. All eight interns learned this fact very fast.

Roger kept a small notebook in his intern blouse pocket which he referred to as, "His brains" meaning, he kept track of useful suggestions and medications in this book as reference items. This effort saved both time and effort in patient care.

Each ward had a chief mogul nurse, some registered nurses, and a cadre of student nurses who had been qualified for ward duty. This system worked well and was efficient.

Roger, after making his ward rounds, went to the X-ray Department to check on any films with the radiologist which had been taken the day before on his patients. This action became another lifetime habit when out in practice. In addition after lunch, he would go to the medical library and spend an hour perusing current medical journals for new information.

These habits were added to his own future medical itinerary. Later on when in practice, he brought the library to himself by purchasing different medical books on specific subjects and/or a number of specialty journals for his study at home.

After lunch, like most interns, Roger went to his quarters to catch a nap. The villain, Mrs. Mason, entered this scene. Knowing intern habits like the back of her hand, she waited until she was sure Roger was asleep; then she called saying, "Doctor, you wrote a order for Mr. Jones for "Hot Packs QID" where would you like those hot packs to be applied? Should my student nurse put them on his feet, abdomen, chest, or where? Please come to the ward and clarify your orders so my students will know what to do."

While grinding his teeth, Roger trudged reluctantly to the ward all the while muttering to himself, "Any moron knows the hot packs should be placed over the sinus areas. Grrr"! Never again did Roger leave any patient's medical orders to speculation, hanging unattached, or to chance as to what he wanted to have instituted. Thanks to "Mother Mason" another trait was etched into Roger's medical armamentarium for a lifetime of use.

Mr. Smith was admitted to the Men's Ward with intermittent abdominal pain, especially, after eating spicy foods. Mr. Smith, upon questioning, described the pain as being a burning and gnawing distress which seemed to center in upper part of the abdomen. There was also a burning discomfort on the right side under his breast bone. These pains seemed to be relieved for awhile by bland foods When Roger palpated a certain area in this part of his abdomen, Mr. Smith flinched and grimaced from the induced discomfort.

A barium x-ray study [UGI] was requested and demonstrated a peptic ulcer near the lower end of the stomach. Medications and a Sippy Diet, which consisted of milk, bland foods, and **NO** spiced items were prescribed. This was the time honored method approach that was recommended in those days.

The Men's Ward contained a heavy load of responsibility for Roger as he was unsupervised most of the time. The volunteer faculty was so busy, because of the War Years and most of the physicians being away in the service, that with their respective heavy practices there was very little time left to make rounds at the med center; consequently, the interns were mostly on their own unless it was a critical situation. Roger thrived on this responsibility and thoroughly enjoyed his role.

Many of the patients were recovering from pneumonia and similar problems. As Roger made his patient rounds, a favorite request by many of the men was, "Doc, I need something for my bowels". [The common remedy was a mixture of "Milk of Magnesia and Cascara"]

A very elderly Dr. Alexander was admitted to the Men's Ward with what known to be a terminal cancerous condition. This doctor had been in practice in a small town all of his life. Roger so enjoyed visiting with him and listening to stories of the physician's life and experiences. Dr. Alexander only lived a short while before he succumbed to a quiet and peaceful demise.

This was Roger's first death, and it had a great impact on him. He learned how susceptible mankind is to different disease processes and sometimes the doctor's hands can only do so much. This was an extremely hard lesson for Roger to endure. Death's finality was such a complete ending event.

From Roger's time on the pediatric ward, he realized that he must learn more about nutrition and how it helped people recover from whatever their illnesses were; so, he asked his fellow interns if they would like a few sessions with the Hospital Dietician. They agreed. Roger proceeded to visit with the dietician, and a time was arranged to meet for several basic sessions which were very informative.

Subsequently, when these sessions were held; all of the interns attended to their great advantage and knowledge. These sessions coupled with what he had learned from his pediatric service, Nutrition became a standard portion of Roger's patient care orders no matter what service that he was in charge of. He, also, became aware of the value to health that was regular exercise, and healthy living habits such as no smoking and limited use of alcohol. He encouraged these traits forevermore.

The interns petitioned Dr. F. Lowell Dunn, who was an excellent internal medicine physician with a PhD in Medical Physiology, to meet with them. He met with the group every Wednesday evening concerning different aspects of medicine and its ramifications. He was a book full of internal medicine information in the cut of Dr. Gedgoud. Boy! How much more Roger had learned at Dr. D's knee. These sessions were one of the big advantages to interning in a teaching hospital. One had to combine the academic with the practical in everyday ward work.

There were several Catholic interns in Roger's group who felt a distinctive lack of knowledge concerning the care of patients in severe/critical health situations. As Roger knew Father Decker S.J. from the days when he was a night student at Creighton University learning about medical ethics, he asked him, "if he would meet with the interns". He did. He would come to the hospital one night a week for almost three months and tutored the group in medical ethics, and the care of the patient in extremis. These lessons were etched in Roger's mind and heart where he carried them for evermore. Roger took this role so seriously that he a wrote a section on the care of a patient in extremis for placement in the "Intern's Manuel'. It was accepted and was so added.

Some of his fellow interns enjoyed teasing Roger about his religion and nicknamed him, "Father King". They frequently engaged him in medical discussions concerning medical ethics. Thanks to his night school at Creighton, he could more than hold his own.

When he would become very irritated and angry, which was not too often, he would turn red in the face; his eyes would pierce like sharp arrows, and an extreme coldness would ensue. When these elements appeared, it was time to leave him alone, and his fellow interns did just that.

Roger frequently mused, As to whether he would really become a worthy doctor and would be able to help his fellowman and do God's work at the same time. Would he be knowledgeable enough to cope with the many, many challenges within this immense field of medicine". He felt so humble and insignificant at times.

His time was up on this service, and he- moved onward to new challenges to the Women's Ward.

CHAPTER 4

THE WOMEN'S WARD

The transition from the Men's Ward to the Women's Ward went very smoothly for Roger. There wasn't much difference in the diseases or examinations experienced between the two genders.

Roger had a new admission of an elderly, matronly lady somewhere in her seventies. Utilizing the interviewing approach that he had developed upon meeting new male patients, Roger approached this lady with the introduction, "Good morning Mrs. Knight I am Dr. Roger King, and I will be looking after you while you are in this hospital". Roger shook her hand and remarked, "I'll bet these hands have seen a lot of events before now." With this greeting, Mrs. Knight visibly relaxed and felt more at ease. She felt some of her many anxieties melt away. Her physician seemed like he was a nice young man and interested in her.

Her chief complaint was that she became nauseous and had marked upper abdominal distress after eating greasy foods. The pain seemed to be the most severe in her upper right quadrant of the abdomen just below the ribs on the right side, and seemed to spread to her back and right wing bone [scapula]. On one occasion, her skin had turned a sickly yellow color, and her eye balls were the same color. She flinched when her abdomen was palpated in this region, but there was no rebound pain as was seen in acute appendicitis. She avoided taking deep breaths due to the discomfort.

Roger scheduled Mrs. Knight for a radio opaque gall bladder study. The day after the studies were completed, he journeyed to the Radiology Department and conferred about the findings with Dr. Hunt, the renowned Radiologist, who was the Chairman of this Department. Dr. Hunt was nationally famous for his treatment of various cancers with irradiation.

Mrs. Wright's study was positive for gall bladder disease and demonstrated several stones in the region of her gall bladder. A surgical consultation was requested and the entire situation of having a cholecystectomy [removal of the gallbladder] was explained in detail by Roger to Mrs. Knight. He assured her that he would be with her at the time of her surgery. With this reassurance, Mrs. Knight was relieved and signed the surgical permission form.

True to form, her surgery went well, and the gallbladder was removed including several stones without any complications. Roger went with her into the operating room and held her hand until the anesthesia took effect.. Fortunately, her post operative period was uneventful. Roger checked on her frequently as he liked her a lot.

After her surgery, she was transferred to the Surgical Ward where other nurses and a different intern cared for her; however, Roger would visit almost daily to observe her post op progress. At last, she was discharged to go home and was able to look after her grandchildren once again. Roger had feelings of nostalgia watching her leave. She thanked him for his kind care and concerns. This heartfelt thanks, made Roger feel glad that he had wanted to become a doctor to help people.

There was another admission to the Women's Ward, a Mrs. Jones, who lately had much difficulty in breathing, coughing, and had some high fevers at times. Roger noticed that during the physical examination, the lady's chest did not raise in a symmetrical manner. There was a lag on the left side with each intake of breath. When he listened to her lungs, the breath sounds were greatly diminished or absent on the left side and when percussed with his fingers, a flat sound was emitted.

Her left lung contained a decrease of breath sounds out near the edge [periphery] of her lung bed. It sounded as though the air was bubbling through water, and there were very fine moist rales [fine watery breath sounds] with crackles being present. Roger concluded that this patient had a pneumonia with considerable fluid in the pleural cavity [a pleural effusion in the space between the lung surface and the rib cage]. Because of her breathing distress, Roger decided that some fluid must be quickly removed before it began to interfered with her heart functions by causing the heart to shift its position and impinge the blood flow to the body.

Roger gave the assisting nurse instructions on doing a thoracentesis [putting a needle into this pleural cavity and removing the fluid] on the left lung. Using a sterile technique of gown, mask, and gloves, Roger remembered that the needle had to be inserted resting on the upper edge of the selected lower rib space. This task was readily accomplished; when the needle was opened, there was "NO Blood or Pus", just a straw colored fluid [pleural effusion]. These findings denoted that the needle was in the right place and not in the lung tissue. About a pint of fluid was drained, and immediately Mrs. Jones could breath much easier.

Roger wrote the rest of the Mrs. Knight's medical orders concerning her treatment regime as her physical situation had been much too acute to do this task before her procedure was performed. She was going to need injections of intramuscular {IM} Penicillin every three hours to conquer the bacteria causing her pneumonia. It needed to be started as soon as possible. Her pneumonia was caused by the wicked and nasty pneumoccocus bacteria. Off to the Hospital Administrator's office Roger hustled, Penicillin was very expensive at this time, and permission had to obtained and justified before it could be utilized.

Permission was given. Mrs. Jones received injections of penicillin every three hours day and night until she was better. It was amazing how well she responded to the penicillin. It was like a miracle compared to the old way of handling pneumonias with temperature control, rest, fluids, and waiting for the temperature crisis to occur. It consisted mostly of supportive care until the body conquered the disease. On the day of her discharge, she thanked Roger profusely. He was beginning to feel like a real doctor at this point in his training. He loved his calling.

He was peacefully sleeping one night for a change when the door bell in his room sounded off. He almost jumped out of his bed. "Shucks! There goes my good night's sleep", thought Roger.

He hustled to the Women's Ward pondering what the problem might be; he found himself confronted by a major one. The new admission was very pale, sweating, writhing in agony lady. Her abdomen was a bit distended. She flinched when Roger put his hand on her abdomen. While listening to it with his stethoscope, the patient's bowels sounded as though they were at war with each other, and there were periodic rushes of these sounds. The first thought that came to Roger's mind was, "Bowel Obstruction". Oh MY! Special x-rays of her abdomen were needed including those of tilting the patient on her side to look for a bowel perforation with air in the abdominal cavity or fluid levels inside the small bowel indicating an obstruction [Left Lateral Decubitus View].

He saw fluid levels in the middle small bowel area and no air in the abdominal cavity. These findings indicated some type of bowel obstruction and needed immediate surgery before the blood supply to the bowel was too impaired as some of the small bowel might be needed to be removed [resected]. A surgical consultation was requested, answered, and Mrs. Jones was on her way to surgery within the wink of an eye.

The surgery was just in time as the bowel was beginning to turn dark and dusky, which meant that the blood flow was impaired and that would mean the loss of some bowel. Post-op, Mrs. Jones was transferred to the surgical ward; and once again, Roger's responsibilities were ended, but he continued to follow her progress until discharge. He learned how important his follow-up of a case was to the patient. They needed a friendly face that they knew and could ask questions. This added lesson, Roger used throughout his medical lifetime. He became to be known as a kindly and concerned doctor who interested in his patients as a human being and not just as another body or disease entity.

The hospital held an outing for the staff, interns, and student nurses at Peony Park Pool and Dance Pavilion. It was a fun affair. Roger was lazily swimming near a long dock which stretched from the shallow water to a much deeper end. Roger had been swimming for years and was like a porpoise in the water. He glanced at the dock and lost his breath, there stood the most extraordinarily beautiful nurse on the deep end of the dock. There were some silly boys horsing around, huffing, puffing, and shoving each other around near her. Roger was about to holler to watch what they were doing when all of a sudden she was catapulted into the water.

She began to flounder around as though she couldn't swim and was panic stricken. Quick as a wink, Roger could see that she could not and was wildly flailing her arms needlessly and gulping water. With a few quick strokes, he was at her side. He could see the sheer panic in her eyes. He was an ex-life guard so he was familiar with the life saving procedures. He gently spoke soothing words to her as he turned her back towards him, grasped her waist, and calmly towed her using a side stroke to shallow water. Finally, they could walk to the beach and sat down where she could breath a great sigh of relief. She was at a loss for words and scared to death.

Roger could see that she was greatly shaken up so he sat beside her and spoke soft inconsequential and reassuring words. He was a very compassionate person. Gradually, Marylou's color came back and her big beautiful eyes lost their fears.

As he sat beside her, she calmed down. He asked how she got to the dock when it was in deep water; learned the beach end was in somewhat shallow water; and she could walk out to that end of the dock. She had been very pleased with her accomplishment. She was watching the swimmers having a delightful time and envied them, so she moved closer to the edge than she should have done.

Roger introduced himself, "By the way, I am Roger King and am an intern at the med center". She replied she was, "Marylou and a junior nursing student at the Center.

She thanked him profusely, "for saving her". Roger went on his way not giving this episode another thought other than what a good looking girl she was and made a vow to look her up very soon.

Marylou began thinking a lot about Roger, and he became sort of a "White Knight" in her mind.; she began to ask her fellow nurses who Roger was and what kind of a person he was. These innumerable questions about Roger caused her compatriots to tease her unmercifully about having a serious crush on him. These goings on were happening to an oblivious Roger.

Unbeknownst to Roger, the nurses began to talk amongst themselves that Roger was becoming a very good and caring physician. Student nurses began to look at him and to find reasons to be seen by him. His eyes were a blue green. He was not handsome, but he had a clean cut and pleasant ambiance. He was a diligent worker, a great listener, very helpful when asked, and exuded compassion and competence. To all of this notoriety, Roger was oblivious. He was unconscious to anything but doing his medical responsibilities. He was pleasant to look at as observed by the nurses. He was five feet ten inches tall, weighed one hundred and sixty pounds, and had straight non-descript brown hair.

Roger was beginning to feel rather claustrophobic as he had not been outside the hospital the for a long time. He was feeling much more comfortable in his role as an intern; so he decided to give himself a break and do something – anything would be better than sitting in the intern quarters bored stiff. He decided that a movie was in order.

Meanwhile, his fellow interns had decided amongst themselves to cover for each other in order to have a few hours of freedom. Roger's luck of the draw indicated that he would be off Tuesday and Thursday evenings and Sunday afternoon and evenings. He would cover for all the others, especially, on Saturday evening as it didn't bother him to be in the hospital on Saturday nights; and the married interns desired that night off.

He remembered in his day dreams about the student nurse, whom he had pulled out of the water on the hospital outing day. She had long, pleasingly black hair, but not quite jet black, and had a prominent widow's peak. Her hair hung to her shoulders. He remembered that she had great big beautiful brown eyes full of expression, which eyes were accented and highlighted by dark eyebrows and very long eye lashes. These features created a lovely frame for her pretty eyes and gorgeous face. She had a clear Celtic porcelain skin which was flawless. Up until now, he had been much too busy to give a thought to having a date. Roger decided that he would take a walk outside and smell the roses for awhile; so he did.

The seasons had changed so much since the last time that he had been outside that he had a hard time believing that there was sunshine, fresh air, blooming colorful flowers, and the sense of freedom awaiting his enjoyment. He resolved to do this more often. In his thoughts, he thought of asking this nurse for a date. He remembered that her name was Marylou, and she was a junior student nurse. Now, if he could only find her.

CHAPTER 5

ORTHOPEDICS AND ENT OUTPATIENT EXPERIENCES

The next step in Roger's training was to spend some time in Orthopedics [Bones]. A great number of Army Doctors were being released from the service and desired some specialty training; so the Med Center began to establish many different residency programs.

The Orthopedic Surgeons on the Voluntary Staff established a Residency Program. A Dr. S. Bach was the first resident to begin this program. Roger really liked him and learned a lot of different procedures and treatments from him from him such as:

1. How to put on a plaster cast
2. How to check a patient's gait and what variations to look for
3. How to set up traction for over-riding bones due to fractures of hips, legs, and/or shoulders
4. How to examine backs for scoliosis and kyphosis in young people [different curvatures of the spine}
5. How to evaluate and treat post polio residual paralysis
6. What to look for in children with cerebral palsy
7. How to reduce a simple fracture of the forearm and the wrist..
8. The usefulness of hot wax treatments to hands for arthritic pains.
9. The evaluation of handicapped children with skeletal deformities
10. Cerebral palsy

Dr Bach was an excellent teacher, and Roger learned considerable practical knowledge about many things under his tutelage.

Dr. Bach told Roger that he should attend the Orthopedic Outpatient Clinic where he learned the way to examine adolescent backs for scoliosis [sideward curvature of the spine] and for kyphosis [forward curving of the spine]. These findings were common among the early adolescent population during their rapid growth periods. This was a fruitful learning experience for his future interest in this age group of young people when in practice.

Lo and behold, the student nurse who was helping with patient care in this clinic was the very attractive girl that Roger had been thinking about. Oh man! She was even more beautiful than he had originally thought. He recalled from the hospital outing that that her name was, "Marylou"; she resided in the nurse's dorm as a third year student in a four year program; this would culminate in a "BS" in Nursing. Roger noticed how carefully she listened to Dr. Bach's explanations to him. He learned that her last name was "Smith". She seemed to be eager to learn, and that, in itself, greatly interested Roger; his thoughts about her spiked even more frequently than before.

In between patients, Roger attempted to make conversations with Marylou She was very polite, but was aloof and only answered questions in a limited manner as though she was not interested in Roger. Actually, she was embarrassed that he might have heard that she was asking about him.

She has great confidence in dating. Her brothers had taught her how to defend herself from undesirable advances. They instructed her to make a tight fist and hit the too amorous character right on the nose, break it, and let the blood spurt. In addition, she was to quickly hit him with a knee in a very sensitive area, watch him writhe in agony; then walk away. She was a very self possess person.

Roger reflected and could see that he had his work cut out for himself if he was going to make any headway with dating her. Roger loved a challenge, and Marylou offered such a challenge. He was looking forward to their next encounter.

Over time, Roger was able to break the ice and learn that she had grown up in St. Patrick's Parish in South Omaha and graduated from South High. As her folks had very little money due to the depression because her father was a brick mason; there was very little work was available for him at that time. Marylou had worked as an usherette at the fancy Orpheum Theatre and, then, as a clerk at the World Insurance Company. She diligently saved her money for her nursing education, which she had always wanted. She was assisted with her tuition with a partial scholarship from the Omaha Medical Center School of Nursing. She was well on her way to achieving her lifelong dream. Roger discovered that she had a sly sense of humor and surprised everyone when she made a "funny".

Roger had an old beat-up Studebaker car which ran most of the time. He finally mustered up enough courage to ask Marylou for a date. She accepted. Unbeknownst to him, she was in seventh heaven because of his asking her out. Roger suggested that they go to the Admiral Theatre which was close by. There was a new movie, "An Affair to Remember" with Cary Grant and Deborah Kerr. Marylou was pleased with this choice, and so they went. The show was so romantic, that before you noticed that it had happened, Mary Lou and Roger were, unconsciously, holding hands. This first time that Roger held her hand, he felt a zinging current coursing through his arm and into his body. This same reaction occurred time and time again whenever he held her hand thereafter. It seemed like magic. Amazing!

Parts of the story were so touching that Marylou had great big salty tears rolling down her pretty cheeks. Roger handed her a clean hankie to wipe the tears away. Marylou was impressed with Roger's thoughtfulness and politeness. He had held the car door open for her while she seated herself. His Mother had trained him well to respect women and to always be courteous.

This was a grand evening out for both of them, and they decided then and there to repeat this outing with another date as soon as they both had the same time off. Roger was in seventh heaven, and Mary Lou began having pleasant dreams about him. His orthopedic service came to an end; so he moved on to the next one.

When Roger was on the ENT Service, he was mostly expected to attend the outpatient clinic where he learned about sinus infections, tonsillitis, and ear infections.

These infections seemed to be never ending and were very plentiful. Ear aches and draining ears were the stable of this clinic, and Roger learned much that would be useful in good stead in the future as a pediatrician. Pediatrics was still his Holy Grail to follow.

Roger learned to examine a child's mouth for a very high arched hard palate as this group of children experienced far more ear infections than those with a flatter palate. The adenoid tissue would partial block the Eustachian Tube [an air canal from the middle ear to the back of the throat]. This air tube was necessary in the air conduction hearing process. This blockage made it difficult for the middle inner ear to drain properly and was a major source of complicating simple ear infections. It frequently led to the undesirable rupturing of the ear drum with an external drainage from the ear.

There were very few ENT in-patients in the hospital; so Roger's experiences were mainly in the outpatient clinic. As part of the rotating internship, it was expected that Roger would perform at least six [6] tonsillectomies and removal of the adenoids [adenoidectomies] while on this six week service. He carefully screened the clinic patients and arranged for the children to have dates for the removal of their tonsils and adenoids. Dr. Lovgren, the attending volunteer faculty member in the ENT Clinic, would supervise the surgery on successive Saturday mornings.

The day came, and Roger geared up his nerve for another new and useful learning experience in the operating room. He put on a scrub suit, donned a surgical cap to cover his hair, and tied a mask using, only, the lower ties. The upper ties would be handled in the operating room. He addressed the sink and began his five minute surgical scrub. When completed, Roger touched the foot pedal of the close by container and doused his hands with alcohol. With his arms held high in the air and being careful not to touch anything, he proceeded into the OR where the room nurse held up a sterile gown so that he could put it on without touching anything. She tied the gown tight and the upper ties of his mask. Roger turned to address the surgical nurse who helped him on with the sterile gloves. They fit snuggly to his fingers so as not to impede his sense of touch.

Following Dr. Lovgren's guidance, he picked up the Adenoid tome with which to remove this tissue. The Adenoid tome was a spoon shaped instrument with many sharp knives contained within the spoon-like area and worked by twisting the handle of this instrument and closing the knives with the removal of the tissue; thusly, the adenoids were removed without any problems. Roger turned to the tonsillar area. He was given a Tonsil Snare, which looked like a wire loop attached to the end of the handle. This loop could be retracted into the handle by twisting the handle, which resulted in cleanly dissecting out the tonsillar tissue.

Any bleeding was controlled by pressure and local cautery on the raw areas. The patient was returned to the pediatric ward bed to be observed for the next forty-eight hours. The children's post-op courses were uneventful. When all six of the tonsillectomies were accomplished, Roger breathed a great sigh of relief. He did not care for surgery of any kind.

Roger continued to spend his designated hour after lunch in the hospital library where he perused the most recent journals. This activity was the beginning of the early stages of Roger's life-long continuing self medical educational program. He unconsciously was imitating his idol, Dr. Gedgoud.

At one of the ENT Clinics, he examined a seven year old boy who had some trouble hearing. His left ear was badly deformed. A light bulb went off in Roger's mind concerning a recent medical article that he had read associating a deformity of the external ear with an associated kidney deformity as these two areas developed in the embryo at the same time. There seemed to be an association between the two deformities.

Roger explained to the child's mother at length about this association and the importance of checking the kidneys for any anomaly. Roger was a very slow, patient, methodical person and very complete with his explanation. He even drew some pictures depicting the various components of the kidney [Renal] system.

Marylou was the nurse who was the designated witness during Roger's explanation of the "What and Why" concerning the need for further studies for the child. She was very impressed about his thoroughness and patience in answering all of the mother's questions, and she had plenty of them. Arrangements were made for an IVP [Intravenous Pyelogram of the kidneys] and a Cystocopy [looking into the bladder with a periscope-like instrument] of the bladder with dye studies of the kidney drainage tubes [Ureters]. The studies were done; and low and behold, they showed a shriveled up non-functioning kidney [atrophied] on one side and what appeared to be a double kidney on the other.

When the mother returned to the clinic, Roger explained the findings in detail to her and that the non-functioning kidney should be removed because of serious future problems that might occur. This Nephrectomy [Removal of the Kidney] procedure was done, and the child recovered without batting an eye.

The word quickly spread throughout the interns and nurse ranks about Roger's astuteness. Other interns began spending more time in the library. Roger's stock went way, way up in the eyes of Marylou, and she hoped that Roger would soon call her for another date.

She conveyed such a polished portrait in her starched white uniform and nursing cap. She was one very attractive lady. She had even, pearly white teeth and a very winning smile that spread across her face like a ray of sunshine peeping through the clouds. Her smile made one feel good all over. She was a very shapely woman in all of the proper place. "What a dish" the fellows thought.

As he was not blind, Roger noticed all of her attributes. It had been quite awhile since he had either talked to or went out with Marylou; so he called her for a date. Unfortunately, she had a very busy social calendar; Roger had to cool his heels and wait his turn. Finally, his turn came on March 1945. They went to Peony Park which had a great danceable band that night. Dancing with Marylou was a real treat and pleasure. She was a great dance partner and was like holding a feather while gliding around the floor. Roger was no slouch, himself. They had a great time.

Roger felt himself becoming attracted more and more to Marylou, and he hoped this attraction was reciprocated. They made it back to the Nurse's dormitory just before her curfew. Roger walked her to the door and as he was telling her what a wonderful time that he had had and that her skin was as soft as the morning dew. Marylou, unexpectedly, kissed Roger; then, quick as wink, she was through the door and was gone before Roger realized what had happened to him. He went home feeling ten feet tall, walking on air with a very full heart. Boy! Was he ever smitten.

Soon Roger's time was up on the ENT Service, and he moved on to the Urology Service.

CHAPTER 6

THE OUTPATIENT UROLOGY SERVICE

Roger entered this new service with a certain amount of reticence as he was not at all interested in this field, but it was part of his training. Again, most of this work was done in the Urology Outpatient Clinic with a few patients needing admission to the hospital for detailed care or for surgery.

In the clinic, he learned to examine men's prostate for irregularities, hard lumps, and general enlargement possibly indicating a cancer or benign hypertrophy. The enlargement of the prostate frequently led to urinary retention with an accompanying major discomfort when trying to urinate. This retention was a big nuisance and created a major urgency to empty the bladder or the need for an emergency catheterization to relive the associated pain.

Amongst the women, he learned that one of their biggest problems and causes of embarrassment was spilling urine when laughing, coughing, or sneezing. This was of great nuisance to them. This situation was due to a cystocoele [a hernial protrusion of a portion of the bladder through the vaginal wall], and had resulted from having several pregnancies with the ensuing trauma to the bladder wall during prolonged labor.

Roger was to assist Dr. Lee with a nephrectomy [removal of a Kidney] for a non-functioning kidney. They scrubbed and gowned for the surgery. When Roger walked into the Operating Room, the patient was already draped with a large green sterile covering including a major opening for performing the surgery. He saw that the various instruments were lined up in military precision on the instrument table which was manned by the gowned and masked Surgical Nurse.

Dr. Lee performed the initial incision. He gave this scalpel to the Nurse and received a new sterile one for the remainder of the procedure. He clamped warm wet towels with large hemostats [clamps used in surgery], and moulded the towels around the wound's edges so that no contamination could occur. Every precaution was taken to prevent any post-op infections from occurring. He proceeded to isolate the right kidney from its surrounding fat pad of tissue.

Roger's job was to hold retractors and to keep the adjacent tissue out of Dr. Lee's way while he worked. He was to clamp off any bleeders which he adroitly did. The intestinal tract was kept pushed out the way by means of warm moist towels.

The kidney was removed without any problem when, at that very moment, Dr. Lee received an extremely urgent call from Methodist Hospital about a major catastrophe. He had to leave immediately. With instructions to Roger to close up the patient, he hustled out the operating room and hurried to Methodist.

The Surgical Supervisor took command of the situation and told the operating nurse to leave the instrument table and become Roger's assistant. She told the circulating nurse to do a five minute scrub and become the surgical nurse. She saw a student passing bye and directed her to become the circulating room nurse.

Roger noted that this student nurse was Marylou. He felt like he was on exhibition and experienced even more anxiety, if that was possible.

Poor Roger! He stood there petrified! What was he supposed to do! There was no one to call for help. He was "IT" big time. Perplexed, Roger rapidly began turning the pages in his mind remembering the layers of the abdomen which needed to be brought together as separate entities. His mind quickly harkened back to his anatomy classes and dissecting the cadaver including the demonstration of the different layers of the abdominal wall.

Anatomy had been one of his favorite subjects during his freshman year. He was one of the top students in his class and was excused from the "Star Chamber of Horrors", the year end examination where there were four anatomy teachers, a blackboard, the cadaver, and the lonely student, who was grilled for well over an hour all alone. This test was the bane of all students, and several did not return at the semester break. Roger had been listed in the "Who's Who of American Universities and Colleges" from his undergraduate days and had later on graduated as an AOA Honor Medical Fraternity member for being in the top ten percent of his class. He was very humble concerning his accomplishments, but he was no dummy.

It was so helpful that previously he had along with the other interns, practiced sewing surgical towels together and working on the art of tying one handed knots.

With these tasks mentally prepared while the nurse was scrubbing, Roger proceeded to clamp bleeding blood vessels with hemostats and to tie off any remaining bleeders. Meanwhile, sweat poured down his back and stood out on his forehead. The circulating room nurse wiped his sweaty brow. To orient himself, Roger began by examining the kidney stump; there was no bleeding; so he proceeded with the abdominal closure.

The surgical nurse slapped a large needle holder containing a slender curved needle with the suture already attached into Roger's hand. He stitched together the inner layer [Peritoneum] of the abdominal wall. This was a moist, serious and flimsy membrane which allowed the intestinal tract to freely move about. He was careful not to traumatize it's surface as it could lead to intraabdominal adhesions.

Next, he proceeded to pull the large, strong abdominal muscles together with tension sutures to alleviate any stress on the incision, itself. The layer just under the skin was the tough, fibrous aponeurosis [tough layer of tissue]. Roger breathed a large sigh of relief when he completed the closure of the skin. Bandages were applied, and the patient returned to the ward for post-op observations and care.

After the patient was returned to the ward and the post-op orders written, Roger sat down to rest his shaking legs and to calm his jumping stomach. Whew! What a horrific ordeal this situation had been! He hoped that such a scenario would never happen again. He was NOT going to be a surgeon, that silly assumption by him was for real. Enough is enough!

Once again, Roger was an unsuspecting hero amidst the nursing corps and grew mightily in Marylou's eyes and estimation. She marveled at how he coolly addressed this unusual experience without seemingly to bat an eye. She wished that he would call her for another date as the last one was so enjoyable even with her embarrassment of spontaneously kissing him good night.

He went merrily on his way never suspecting any of the conversations going on behind his back or having knowledge of Marylou's feelings. He was oblivious to this post surgical adulation. Roger carried a very unassuming nature. He just wanted to be the best doctor that he could be.

The remainder of Roger's Urological Service was uneventful. Thank heavens! On to the Anesthesia Service!

CHAPTER 7

THE ANESTHESIA SERVICE

Roger reported to the operating suits early on a Monday morning for another opportunity to learn new procedures and duties. Dr. Macintosh met him and took him under his wing to show him the ropes of anesthesia. Dr. Mac was a part time anesthesiologist and worked as a Radiologist at another hospital after the morning's surgical schedule was completed. He was on the Volunteer Faculty at the Med Center.

Mostly Ether was utilized, as the anesthetic of choice, but sometimes an explosive gas, Cyclopropane, was administered. Occasionally, an intravenous medication, sodium pentothal, was used depending upon what the surgeon desired, and the type of surgery being performed..

Dr. Mac and Roger did a surgical scrub each morning in preparation before starting anything. This habit stayed with Roger all the rest of his life. He always started his day by scrubbing his hands with a brush for a few minutes even when he was out in the real world.

Patients were due. His role was to assist them into the operating room, help them onto the operating table, and explain what he was going to be about. The surgeon was the reining authority in the operating room; his word was law and decided what anesthesia he wanted to be administered; so it came to pass.

The current case was a simple appendectomy. Dr. Cochran was the chief surgical resident. He had been a. Colonel in the Army Medical Corp and had assisted in developing the "Mash Mobile Hospital Units" which were so successful in saving many lives during World War II as the Unit was located very close to the front lines. Being so located, it cut down on the resulting shock due to the delay of transporting a wounded soldier to first class care.

Dr. Cochrane was very bossy and had forgotten that he was not in the armed service any more. He and Roger did not hit it off very well. Roger did not like surgery or bossiness, and let people know his preferences. Any indifference to surgery was a mortal sin to Dr Cochran.

Roger applied the Ether drip; the patient went to sleep;, and the operation proceeded on schedule. It was uneventful. The patient was returned to his ward for his post-op care. Dr. Cochran was determined to show who was boss when Roger came onto the surgical service. He wouldn't be allowed to do much surgery as he stated unequivocally.

Dr. Cochran doled out the simple appendectomies and hernia repairs to his favorites; and, obviously, Roger was not one of them. Roger was irritated by this attitude; and any way, he didn't care about doing any surgery. He could give away any of his opportunities for all he cared to someone that was more interested. This attitude irritated Dr. Cochran even more, like rubbing salt into a wound.

Meanwhile, Roger was feeling closed in again as he hadn't been out of the hospital since his wonderful date with Marylou. Would she even remember him? He had noticed that she had been drafted to work in the operating room where he had sweat blood. He cranked up his nerve and called her. Unfortunately, she was busy this particular night, but they talked on and on like a pair of old friends learning more about each other.

Roger was so enamored with Marylou and having conversations with her that he would call her about 9:00 pm on many nights. She did not seem to mind his calling so often, in fact, she began to look forward to them, and was disappointed when he didn't call. He would phone from the darkened surgical area where the lighting was dim and privacy was insured. Privacy was not possible in the intern quarters, besides, those phone lines could not be tied up for very long. His talks with Marylou seemed to stretch out over a longer and longer period of time. He so enjoyed hearing the sound of her voice that he was reluctant to hang up.

Roger thought about Mary Lou more and more each day and greatly appreciated her very enticing figure as he was not a celibate monk. On the basis of a one to ten scale, her curvaceous figure rated at least an eleven. She was great wolf whistling material and was subjected to it frequently when away from the hospital environs. She was a petite lady about five feet three inches and weighted near one hundred and five pounds. In other words, she was quite a "Delightful Sight" to behold.

Roger had been taught by his Mother and two older sisters to respect women, which he did. He still had not come down to earth since she had spontaneously kissed him after the romantic movie, and had dashed into her dormitory in embarrassment before he could say a word. Back to work!

On one occasion, there was a burn patient with extensive burns over his face and upper torso. An inhalation anesthetic was impossible so IV Sodium Pentothal was the anesthetic of choice. While Roger was preparing the patient for the anesthetic, his mind kept drifting to Marylou, and when he might have another date with her. He was really smitten without any doubt. "Get back to work", His mind told him; and so he did.

The patient was draped, and all Roger had was an arm to use for the IV anesthetic. Any glimpse of the patient's face was purely coincidental. Being able to observe the patient's features in order to check his color or other manifestations, that held the needed signs concerning how the patient was progressing and tolerating the procedure, became purely happenstance. This situation put him, and the patient at a distinct hazardous disadvantage. Dr. Cochran kept telling Roger to give the patient more anesthetic, as he was moving a bit because this inherently created problems with the work on the patient's face.

As a result of the added Sodium Pentothal, the patient did not awaken as soon as expected. Roger sat for the next two hours breathing for the patient by compressing the inhalation bag to force oxygen into his lungs. Finally, he began to rouse from the depths of the anesthesia. Thank heaven!

Because of the seriousness of this situation consisting of poor supervision of an inexperienced intern, Drs. Dorothy Thompson and Muriel Francesca were hired on a part time basis to supervise when interns were giving any type of anesthesia. The interns welcomed this change. Meanwhile, Roger's patient had recovered without any discernible aftermath. He breathed a deep sigh of relief with this outcome. He told Marylou about this experience; she sympathized and comforted him concerning his anxieties.

Roger was very glad when this ordeal was over as he did not feel comfortable during the entire patient's debridement [removal of the destroyed tissue] of the facial skin. The patient did very well to Roger's great relief.

Dr. Cochran took photographs of his burn patients in preparation for any skin grafting that might be necessary in the future. He was one of the first surgeons to document his work via film for future comparisons. He was an excellent photographer.

Now, it was time to move onto the next service which unfortunately for Roger was surgery, and Dr. Cochran awaited his coming with relish and obvious glee. He would show Roger who was in charge.

CHAPTER 8

THE SURGICAL SERVICE

Doctor Anderson was the volunteer surgeon on call when an appendectomy was scheduled for surgery. Roger was the intern assigned to assist him. After the patient was draped and anesthetized, Dr. Anderson told Roger to come over to the surgeon's side and do this procedure.

Roger could literally hear Dr. Cochran's teeth grinding in a real fit of pique. Roger smiled to himself and felt great that he could irritate and disrupt Dr. Cochran's plans for him. Just for the record, this sequence of activities occurred several times in the future much to Dr. Cochran's dismay and disgust.

Dr. Cochran had a slender form and hawk-like piercing eyes peering out from under hooded lids. Humor was his short suit. He had an abrasive laugh and voice tones.

This patient's surgical area had been painted with a red antiseptic solution. This material left a brown tinge to the skin. The patient was draped with sterile sheets containing a large hole for making the incision. Roger made the initial incision and handed this knife to the Instrument Nurse and received a sterile one in return. He proceeded to clamp surgical towels over the lips of the incision. The abdomen was opened with just a few slices of the knife. He located the appendix, handled it with great care, and cautiously isolated it from the surrounding tissues by moist sterile towels. He clamped a forceps at the base of the appendage. The clamp went click, click as the jaws were closed. Another forceps was placed just above the other one with a small space in between.

It was imperative that the appendix not burst and cause a major peritonitis within the abdominal cavity; that catastrophe happening would be very damaging to the patient's chance of survival. The entire surrounding area was packed with hot moist towels.

Roger applied a purse string suture above and one below the appendix pedicle, itself. An incision was made between the two sutures and clamps. The knife was discarded; the appendix was separated from the lower end of the ascending colon. This specimen was sent to the laboratory for analysis. The remaining stump of the appendix attached to the large bowel [Cecum] was cauterized, and the patient was closed in the usual manner. The incision was dressed. The patient returned to his ward for post-op observation and care.

Roger breathed a sigh of relief as he removed his gloves and gown. Doctor Anderson congratulated him on a job well done while Dr. Cochran continued to grind his teeth. "There won't be many teeth left if he keeps that up', thought Roger, with a sadistic hidden grin.

Roger assisted at many different procedures, but never came to like or relish surgery as some of the interns did. He was firmly committed to pediatrics and didn't mind the snide remarks or the eye rolling behind his back about desiring to care for "Babies" and be a "Baby Doctor". Pediatrics was very low in estimation on the totem pole amidst many of the medical specialties in a multitude of minds. However, it was a very mind challenging medical specialty and the powers of observation needed to be finely honed..

Another new patient was admitted to the surgical ward from a very traumatic car accident. Roger examined the female pronto. As he placed a hand on her abdomen, he noticed that it was as rigid as a board. The patient had very shallow breathing, a rapid pulse, sweat beads were forming on her forehead, and she had left shoulder pain, which Roger surmised came from pressure below the diaphragm. The first thoughts that came to Roger's mind was, "This must be a ruptured spleen". He immediately called Dr. Cochran who came in haste and ordered surgery at once. At the time of the surgery, the abdomen contained much blood from the traumatic blow to her abdomen. The surgery was difficult, but successful; she was returned to the surgical ward for post-op care.

With great reluctance, Dr. C. praised Roger for his astute diagnosis. They began to develop a better repoire, which improvement became, once again, the talk of the nursing corps. Meanwhile, Roger was oblivious about their admiration. Marylou had developed very warm feelings towards Roger and hoped that he would call for another date as they had had so much fun on the last one.

Perforated ulcers, gallbladder removals [cholecystectomy], hernia repairs were some of the procedures that Roger had assisted with while working at the operating table. Soon, his time on surgery was over, and he moved onto the OB and GYN Service. He was glad to leave Dr. Cochran with his muted antagonism behind and go onto greener pastures.

CHAPTER 9

THE OB AND GYN SERVICE

Fortunately, Dr. Willis Taylor was back from the Navy and was the occupant of the newly established OB-GYN Residency position. He was a great likeable teacher. His father was a prominent OB-GYN physician in the city. In fact, he had delivered Roger in major snow storm some twenty-four years previously. Because of the calendar and the way the various Medical Services had been constructed, there was three months left in the internship in order to put the scholastic calendar back onto a July to June basis. Roger would be serving his remaining three months on this particular Service. He looked forward to it as preparation for his love of pediatrics and this field's effect on newborns. This love had grown from mere thoughts of pediatrics as a lifetime venture into a full blown passion for the specialty. He was anxious to learn all different facets of this field.

Roger worked in the OB-GYN Outpatient Clinic as well as on the ward. He learned how to calculate a mother's gestational time to delivery and how to do a pelvic examinations under Dr. Taylor's tutelage. He was responsible to deliver the simple and uncomplicated deliveries. He learned the various stages of a mother's labor and acquired excellent resuscitation techniques for those infants who did not desire to breath right after birth. Mastering these skills was no mean feat; Roger used what he had learned on this service throughout all the rest of his professional life.

As usual, a baby decided, itself, when it was ripe enough and ready to go out into the cold cruel world; commonly, this frequently seemed to occur at 2:00 am in the morning. Roger was called at this hour one fine night. He checked the mother's stage of labor and knew she was due to deliver very shortly. He told the nurses to prep the mother while he gowned and gloved. This was done.

The mother was bearing down and having major contractions. Roger saw the crowning of the head, but the head seemed to need a larger opening to come forth into the world. Though he had seen it done before, he had never performed an episiotomy, himself. The nurse handed him a pair of scissors, and the necessary outlet cut was made. The baby slid easily into Roger's waiting hands. The infant came into the world with a loud slippery and slurping sound and with an extremely loud cry. The baby's throat was aspirated of any mucus and handed over to the nurse to show to the mother. She was all smiles as she held her first born. Roger was elated that his delivery went so smoothly. He was so smitten with new life anytime he delivered an infant. Now, all he had to do was to repair the episiotomy which he did skillfully, once again recalling his anatomy details. He was in awe of the birth of any child all through his lifetime.

Roger delivered many babies while on this service. Dr. Taylor's Father had a sudden and massive heart attack. Dr. Taylor endeavored to hold his father's practice together while still being a resident. This was a mighty task to undertake. Consequently, the burden of running this service fell on Roger's shoulders while the young Dr. Taylor tried to be in two or more places at once as he had major tasks on his hands. Roger rose to the occasion and handled the Service with great skill and common sense with just marginal help from his resident.

Roger handled the OB Outpatient Clinic and the OB Ward with ease. Each mother, when being discharged, had to have a physical including a vaginal exam prior to her discharge. This task did not thrill him. Another unpleasant tasks was the treatment of venereal warts [condyloma acuminata – human Papillomavirus] – which needed to be painted with a podophyllumn cauterizing solution. These warts were precursors for different types of genital cancers, especial cervical cancer, and were seen frequently in sexually active adolescents.

While on this service, one day there appeared in his mail box a letter from the Surgeon General's Office of the Army Medical Corps. It explained that the Service needed some partially trained medical specialists and was offering the opportunity to spend one additional year in training before fulfilling the two year obligation. Roger, immediately, went to see Dr. Gedgoud as to what institutions he should apply for a pediatric residency. Dr. Gedgoud suggested Roger consider staying here at the med center as dirt was just being dug for the new Childrens' Hospital and would be in use before Roger had to report for duty.

This advice seemed like manna from heaven, and Roger agreed. Dr. Gedgoud talked with Dr. Henske, the Voluntary Head of Pediatrics, about the feasibility of a pediatric residency. Dr. Henske thought it was a good idea and wanted to interview Roger This was accomplished. Dr. Henske asked Roger one very significant question, "Do you want to work?" Roger answered, "I have never been afraid of hard work or long hours; so the answer is "Yes"; and so it came to pass. Roger was on his way to live his heart's desire and dreams.

He could hardly wait to tell Marylou of his good fortune. She was very pleased as she dreaded the thoughts of Roger leaving Omaha. She had come to like him very much. He was occupying a very special spot in her heart. She was in the early phases of falling in love. He seemed to be constantly in her inner most thoughts.

They celebrated his good fortune by going to the Orpheum Theatre to see Mickey Rooney and Ann Miller in "Sugar Babies". After parking the car, they walked hand in hand to the show and held them all during the performance. He had all sorts of wonderful and warm thoughts while holding Marylou's hand. He felt the magic flow from her hands into his as they sat watching the show. Roger was totally and completely smitten with Marylou. His heart was overflowing; he had trouble not telling her his feelings so she wouldn't become frightened and dump him.

Life was so good! Being old fashion and with great respect for females and when they arrived back at the nurse's dormitory, he asked, "Could kiss her goodnight". She told him, "I had hoped that you would". Their kiss was a prolonged one as their tongues did a tango. He thought her skin was so fair, porcelain in nature, and very Celtic in appearance. Her lips were warm and tasty when he brushed them against his; she felt her world tilt; then, right itself as only real sweethearts would know how it happened. Roger walked on air all the way back to the intern quarters.

With Marylou, it was perfect when he held her in his arms. In her mind, this was everything that dreams are made of. At that moment in time, she became his totally and undeniably. She felt a great feeling of ease as she accepted these feeling into her inner most being.

Meanwhile, the work on the OB Service continued. Roger examined a mother in the first stage of labor and thought the placenta was in the wrong place; and that it lay across the opening of the womb [placenta previae]. If a placenta separated from the womb before delivery, the mother could bleed profusely endangering her life and the infant's, big time. Time was of an essence. This situation was a dire emergency.

He called Dr. Taylor, who was in his father's office and explained the situation. Dr. Taylor came, checked the patient, agreed, and told the operating supervisor to set up for an emergency Cesarean Section. This was done. A fine baby girl was delivered, and the placenta was found to be across the mouth of the uterus. Once again, the nurses noted how astute Roger was, and the word spread everywhere that he was rounding into a fine doctor.

Marylou heard about Roger's professional acumen and called to let him know her joy. This put Roger into ecstasy. "She must like me a bit", he thought.

As part of the GYN Service, the intern had to remove any radiation needles which had been put in place by Dr. Hunt for treatment of cancer of the cervix. This removal had to be precise day or night without fail; so too much irradiation would not occur. This job was a messy, smelly, stinky task due to the odor of the necrotic tissue from the irradiation. No one liked to do this task, but it was all in a day's work. Not all aspects of medicine are wine and roses he determined.

Being on the OB Service brought back old experiences to Roger's mind that when he was a junior med student and on the home delivery service. This activity occurred during the summer months and was a volunteer program. Dick Kalmanson was his partner. When a call came that a mother was in labor, the two of them proceeded to the OB Clinic, picked up the packs of sterile materials, and Ms. Braun, who was a certified midwife. She would be supervising the delivery.

They drove to a dingy home in East Omaha which was filled with trash, debris and a lots of dirt. It was hard to find a fairly clean spot where one could sit. What an amazing experience this was for Roger and Dick to see how some indigent folks did not live, but merely struggled to exist. After checking the mother, it was noted that she was at a level three stage of labor; so it would be awhile before the delivery. Ms. Braun checked and confirmed their assessment. When it was time for the delivery, the packs of sterile supplies were opened, and the mother prepped with soap and water. She delivered a darling little girl. Roger and Dick were very much impressed and so proud doing this delivery. It was such an enlightening experience, that they volunteered for another turn as there were so few volunteers to cover the summer months.

On another occasion while on the OB Service, Roger checked a mother with early contractions and severe abdominal pain in her lower abdomen. After checking her, he thought she might have a ruptured tubal pregnancy. Dr. Taylor confirmed his diagnosis, scheduled surgery, and removed the mother's right Fallopian Tube containing the pregnancy. Sometimes a tubal pregnancy ruptured like this one, and the mother could bleed profusely endangering her life. Her post-op course was uneventful; except for her post op depression upon losing her Fallopian Tube, and its possible effect on having future pregnancies. Roger spent a considerable amount of time consoling and reassuring the mother that the world had not come to an end, and that she probably could have future pregnancies still having the other tube.

Roger became very adept at consoling disconsolate folks. Noting this gift, the nurses frequently asked him to visit with grieving patients, who were not his patients. The nursery personnel would call upon him when an infant was in dire trouble in order to baptize the infant before any priest or minister could be located. There were no hospital chaplains in those early days.

The crowning touch to Dr. Cochran's dilemma came one day when Roger was to assist Dr. Finlay with a hysterectomy due to severe bleeding from uterine fibroids. Dr. Finlay told Roger to come to the surgeon's side of the table to perform this procedure. He would be both his assistant and his mentor. Poor Dr. Cochran was beside himself because Roger had been doing so much surgery. He had no way to stop it. In spite of his dislike of surgery, Roger was adept and ended up doing more procedures than most of his fellow interns. He proceeded to do the procedure. He had done so many different ones that he would no longer quail with the thoughts of surgery.

The uterus is a pear shaped organ in the pelvis supported by two broad ligaments along with the Fallopian Tubes which carried the eggs from the ovary to the uterus where possible fertilization occurred. The uterus, but not the ovaries, was the object of this surgery. The Tubes were clamped, cut, and ligated. The uterine arteries were identified, and secured with double ties. The entire uterus was removed and sent to pathology for study.

There was a huge fibroid in the uterus which caused all of the trouble. It was imperative that no raw areas be left behind; so the stump of the uterus needed to be covered by a layer of peritoneal tissue so adhesions could not form and possibly be the cause of tying up the bowel with an obstruction. This problem might happen later on any time during the patient's ensuing lifetime. Dr. Finlay congratulated him on a job well done.

He was extra careful not to crush any tissue as that could be a fertile field for an infection or adhesions to develop. In a few days, he checked with the pathology department. They determined that it was a very large fibroid only, and no cancer cells were found.

Roger, later on, found out that he was the first intern to ever perform a hysterectomy in the history of the med center. Wow! Poor Dr. Cochran was beside himself with irritations, Big Time! Roger gave himself a very smug smile.

Roger's internship drew to a close and it was on into his Pediatric Residency program. He moved out of the intern quarters and into a small one room apartment close to the med center. He soon learned that he would be swimming in financial wealth as his new stipend would be forty dollars per month plus board. Oh My!

PART 2

ROGER KING M.D. - RESIDENT

THE MOLDING OF A PEDIATRICIAN

CHAPTER 10

A NEW BEGINNING

Roger was having very serious thoughts about desiring to marry Marylou. They talked and talked and compared their many likes and dislikes. They discovered that they had many interests in common. Roger would send Marylou silly love letters put together with words and pictures cut out of magazines. She was amused by his ingenuity and persistence, and began having serious thoughts about him as well. Sensing this change in interest towards him, Roger pushed his quiet courtship in earnest

One evening after a date, Roger looked into her beautiful eyes and was lost in their deep brown abysses. He told Marylou that he was having a hard time sleeping, waking up all hot and sweaty, and having exotic dreams mostly about her. During the day, everywhere he gazed, he would see her face or hear her voice even if she wasn't there. He was beginning to worry and fret about these thoughts. He had the sensation that something was the matter with him and maybe he should see a psychiatrist.

"Well", said Marylou, "That's sounds like a very serious malady to me. It certainly is a great cause for concern. From my own extensive nurse's training, I know of only one cure for such a major condition". "What is that" asked Roger? As soon as I graduate from Nursing School, you will just have to marry me and that will provide a long term solution to your concerns".

Roger could not believe his ears or eyes. There she was all soft, beautiful, and delectable, just as serious as all get out, looking at him with her big beautiful brown eyes waiting for an answer. He replied, "With these dire symptoms of mine, I believe that your diagnosis is right on the button; and the only treatment course for me is to follow out your suggestions. Should I ask your father for your hand"? inquired Roger, who was of the old traditional school concerning protocols. Marylou laughed and replied, "There is no need as this is the twentieth century and I am my own liberated woman and make my own decisions".

With that statement, he grabbed her and covered her with all kinds of kisses, strokes, and hugs. Time stood still; both hearts were pounding like trip hammers. After awhile their hearts settled down to a quiet purr and a more normal rhythm. He whispered in her ears, "I love you so, and I always will". His hands slid up her neck holding her close to his lips while he kissed her again and again. Her lips had a silky texture and tasted like ambrosia – very delectable. The flavor of her tongue would linger with him for days to come. Meanwhile, their tongues did a rapid tango together. His heart thundered under the feel of her hands. When they kissed, her breath came with soft sighs and moans of pleasant joy. Whenever Marylou spoke, it seemed it seemed as if time was old as yesterday and yet as new as tomorrow; her voice had such a bell-like quality. Whenever

Roger held her, he could hear and sense a hundred harp strings melodiously sailing on the winds. He was truly smitten.

Roger was in such ecstasy that his feet barely touch the ground. Whenever he kissed her, Roger heard bells ringing and fireworks going off in his head. Her soft arms winding around him would glide with great wonderment as they slid up and down his back, and created within him the sensations of sheer delight. He felt as though he was in heaven on earth. He wanted to give her everything – his heart, mind, body, and the moon. His ambition was to keep her safe from harm and immensely happy forever more. He told her, "You are everything to me".

Marylou laughed and returned his kisses with great ardor. She ran her fingers through his hair and held him tight to her body. Roger felt his hands caressingly go up and down her arms and back as though he couldn't touch her enough for fear that she would evaporate and that he would wake up from a beautiful dream. He had to force himself to stop kissing her. Marylou laughed and said," Hey! Save some of those tasty treats for another time. I am not going anywhere without you". As she laughed in joy, Roger thought her laughter sounded like the tinkling of a thousand bells or the musical warbling of a flock of song birds. He felt that he had had a glimpse of heaven. No matter how hot their passion was, they both were innocent and remained so. The over whelming depth of her love for Roger moved her heart to beat to a timed tempo of the ages.

Marylou exuded such a sense of supreme competence that Roger knew that she would help him throughout their lifetime together. It created a very heady feeling within him. He was realizing what an exceptional person she was. He doted on these feelings whenever he was away from her. He was so pleased that she would belong to him and he to her.

Marylou heard her sister nurses talking about what a great Roger guy seemed to be and had cultivated their interest. She decided to nip these thoughts in the bud and told them, "Hey! He is mine! All mine! Back off and go concentrate on someone else". They did that with great reluctance.

He walked with his head in the clouds seemingly forever. Her graduation would be in only two months. Roger went to see his old friend from long ago, Al Kraus, a jewelry repair artist, and asked him to obtain a suitable wedding ring set for him. Roger cashed in his War Bonds and had $700 available for the rings. Al did Roger a big favor. He obtained, at cost, an outstanding wedding ring of platinum containing several small diamonds with a matching lovely engagement ring containing a fairly large diamond and side diamonds. The rings were beautiful to behold.

At their next date, Roger knelt down on one knee and formerly asked Marylou to be his wife forever more. She said, "Yes". He slipped the gorgeous engagement ring on her finger and sealed it with a long and hearty kiss. Once again, their tongues danced a merry whirl of delight; thereafter, they would bill and coo like a pair of love birds. The low and soft sound of his voice had her mind floating on a sea of happiness.

On Monday morning, he had to come back to reality and start his first day of his new residency program.

It seemed just like yesterday when he walked onto the pediatric ward as an intern for Dr. Gedgoud's rounds, for the first time. Today, a new intern was to be the recipient of Doctor's questions and interrogations. Roger would listen carefully and formulate an answer to the question in his own mind as he was so anxious to learn everything that he could. Dr. G was such an outstanding and amazing teacher. Every once in a while, Dr. G. would try to catch Roger off balance and ask him a direct question. Fortunately, Roger was wise to this game and was able to answer correctly the question which response pleased Dr. G no end.

At times, Roger was committed to teach a group of student nurses, who were assigned to the pediatric floor. He spoke about the importance of observing the patient for any changes from the previous day; and the necessity for accuracy in writing the nursing notes on a child's chart as their observations were the doctor's eyes and ears when he wasn't present. Roger enjoyed this exercise very much as it helped him to cement many concepts in his own mind.

He found that teaching about an infant's and a child's natural growth and development processes provided an immense and serious attraction for him. While in the library, he pursued many different texts and articles concerning this topic and associated ones. He became an ardent student of Dr. Arnold Gesell, who studied how children grew and changed by utilizing serial and periodic movies of children growing, playing, and changing. Dr. Gesell had authored many books on this subject. Roger was an apt pupil and student of his theories. He obtained copies of these books for his own library, which he used extensively in his future years.

Dr. G gave lectures to junior medical students on the value of the different growth charts which were available for following a child's height and weight changes. Dr. G especially liked the "Wetzel Grid" for many reasons. Roger was so intrigued by this chart that he used it exclusively from thence forth when he was in the army and beyond in what would be his future medical practice.

There was a Swiss Psychologist, Piaget, who studied the processes by which children discovered and learned; once again Roger was an apt pupil. He studied all of his works. He read every article in the library that he had published. The more extensively he read and studied, the more Roger incorporated these principles into his everyday thinking. Little did he realize that in the distant future he would see Dr. Piaget in person at a medical meeting based upon the theme of children's' growth and development.

Dr. G gave lectures to the junior students on the physical development of children; Roger arranged his schedule so he could attend these critical lectures. He was like a sponge thirsting for knowledge. Inherently and sub conscientiously, Roger began formulating the foundation of his future pediatric practice based upon keeping well children well via immunizations and well child guidance based upon the principles he was learning from these three outstanding sources. In the future, he would utilize the term, "Guided Growth" as his mantra for the "Well Child Advice" to be given within his practice and in participating in many different lectures to groups. This advice was based upon the "Clues" the child would exhibit and was geared to each child's own personal growth and development.

In addition to the State Board Examination, he elected to take the National Board of Medical Examinations. These later exams consisted of a written test and an oral examination at the conclusion of his internship. These Boards were accepted in many more states than the Nebraska ones. During his oral examination, he met a unique pediatrician, Dr. Tompkins knew so much about the emotional growth of children, and the "Clues" they exhibited. These "Clues", would indicate the next phase of development inherent in an infant or child. Roger rapidly grasped the value of this approach and made it an integral part of his armamentarium.

For example: "When is the appropriate time to introduce solid foods into an infant's diet, instead of the old fashioned and arbitrary time of six months"? The answer would be, "Whenever the infant's "Tongue Thrust" stops pushing food out of its mouth, and the tongue could actively carry food to the back of the throat for swallowing purposes". Parental advice was geared to these different and many "Clues".

These were simple but important observations and were the key to adapting the real world to the infant's physiological development. Dr. Tompkins's philosophies made a lot of common sense to Roger; so he began to attend on his own these child development talks. Doctor T. gave these classes solely to his private practice parents on Saturday afternoons.

Roger was busy taking in, storing away, and incorporating into his own philosophies of growth and development everything he could. He was bound and determined that he would become an excellent pediatrician bar none. He never worried about his future and making a lot of money; as he knew that success and monetary security would follow the trail of supreme excellence; and so it came to pass.

Roger worked with all the interns on their pediatric service to help them learn, especially, about a child's growth and development. One day a smart-alecky intern said to him, "King, you don't know what you are talking about when it comes to children! How many children do you have? I have six, and I know that you have none"! Well! Those remarks cut deep, hurt, and not so gently put Roger in his place. Those comments made him feel very humble with his teaching, and renewed his studies with even greater vigor. Mentally, he thanked that intern many times over.

Two months had passed, and Marylou's graduation loomed just over the horizon. She was in the middle of the final tests for her State Nursing Boards; in addition, to the preparations for their wedding. She had a very full plate to handle. Patiently, Roger tried to stay out of her way so as not to cause any needless stress, worries, or concerns. He just helped with morale support.

She aced her Boards and was hired by the Med Center to work in the newborn nursery. She was ecstatic that she would be working in Roger's field.

Graduation Day came. The class of nurses were all dressed in their starched white uniforms and specific school caps. They were very impressive en masse. Each nurse walked across the stage, had their cap ceremonially adjusted, and received their diploma. Roger was so proud of Marylou that the buttons on his shirt threatened to pop off. Just as it happened at his graduation, all the nurses stood and recited the impressive "Nightingale Pledge":

> *I solemnly pledge myself before God and in the presence of this assembly to pass my life in purity and to practice my profession faithfully.*
>
> *I will abstain from whatever from what is deleterious and mischievous, and will not take or knowingly administer any harmful drug.*
>
> *I will do all in my power to maintain and elevate the standard of my profession and will hold in confidence all personal matters committed to my keeping and all family affairs coming to my knowledge in the practice of my calling.*
>
> *With loyalty will I aid the physician in his work, and as a missioner of health, I will dedicate myself to devoted service for human welfare.*[2]

---

[2] Nightingale Pledge from Wikipedia, the free encyclopedia

The ceremony ended with a sigh of pleasant satisfaction and relief. Graduation came and went, the many parties and celebrations ended. It was back to the real world, and whatever new adventures were hiding just around the next corner.

Meanwhile, the wedding preparations went full steam ahead. Marylou's three sisters were an integral part of the planning. Her older sister, Josie, would be her maid of honor. Roger really liked her. The other two were OK but didn't greatly impress him. The youngest sister, Tessie, kept giving Marylou a hard time for getting married and disrupting their concepts of being "Little Women" as in the book of the same name. When they were little, they often played the roles that were the characters in this story.

Roger and Marylou went hunting for a larger apartment as the one he had was living in a small cracker box. They found one not too far from the Med Center; so they could walk to work.

When the great December Wedding Day came and was filled with anxieties, Roger entered St. Patrick's Church. He was struck with the solemnity and holy atmosphere present. He absorbed the serenity that it portrayed. The lights were dimmed, the candles were flickering, and there was the sweet odor of the flowers mixed with the pungent smell of incense awaiting the ceremony. The church had been decorated beautifully for the Christmas holidays.

Marylou's dress was her sister "Fifi's" [Genevieve}, "May Queen Crowning Gown" from her high school days. Her Mother had altered it to fit Marylou's delightful curves. She was more petit than her other sisters. She was only five foot three and weighed about one hundred and eight pounds. She was a delightful armful. Marylou was the second oldest girl in the family next to her sister, Josie.

Marylou looked at her father, and thought that he was so handsome. She noticed several tears glistening on his eye lashes. She gently nudged him with her elbow and whispered, "NO crying allowed on my special day! Stop that!" and so he did. Her father thought to himself, "I am giving away part of my heart, and it hurts".

Roger could hardly believe his eyes when Marylou started to walk down the aisle on her father's arm. She was a dream come true. Her beauty shown like a beacon from afar. Her long black hair curled around her shoulders, her brown eyes were framed above by her dark eye brows, and below, her eyes themselves were rimmed with long curling eye lashes. She was a sight to behold. This picture was etched forever in his mind to be revisited on many occasions in their future years together.

Roger was filled with wonderment that Marylou was going to be his and his alone forever. He silently thanked the good Lord for his long desired goal of marrying a wonderful Catholic girl where they would be able to pray and play together in unison.

After they said their vows of everlasting love, the two of them walked to a side alter of the Blessed Mother where they lighted, simultaneously, a single candle signifying symbolically that they were two persons, now, in one.

After the wedding, the group adjourned to the Regis Hotel for the wedding breakfast which was filled with many loving and amusing toasts to the couple. Father Saxon, her pastor and the one who married them, was included. There had been no bachelor dinner for Roger due to cost factors; any way, most of his friends were away in the service.

During the evening after the wedding, there was a small, intimate reception at Marylou's home with her fellow usherettes from the Orpheum, nursing school friends, and a few other close friends. Roger's oldest sister, Fannie, by ten years, came from the

State of Washington for the ceremony. She had been like a second mother to him much to his eternal consternation. His other sister and Mother could not come due to job restrictions.

As they were married on a Saturday and had to be back to work on Monday, their honeymoon consisted of one night, only, in the Cornhusker Hotel in Lincoln, Nebraska. When the check-in clerk learned that they had just been married, he changed their reservations to the Bridal Suite complete with champagne at no extra cost. Their real honeymoon would have to wait until sometime later.

As both were stanch Catholics, they utilized the natural rhythm method of birth avoidance rather than the artificial methods of contraceptive prevention. If a pregnancy resulted, they would deal with the outcome without any qualms. Any infant would be welcomed with open arms.

This fact did not phase either of them. They would be together through thick and thin for evermore. Their honeymoon night was spent in the joyful bliss of exploring the wonders, mysteries, and delights of each other's bodies, and they made love several times during the night. When he kissed her, passion would cloud her senses.

* * * * *

CHAPTER 11

A NEW WORLD OF EXPLORATION

One day, Dr. Gedgoud told Roger to come with him; they walked across the street to the Child's Savings Institute, where he explained to Roger that he would be doing physical examinations on about twenty infants weekly. The exams were for a special study to determine, "Whether or not the early feeding of infants with the newly developed Baby Meat products would keep the natural drop in the red blood count which occurs between birth and about five months of age, from happening". A fellow resident in pathology would be doing weekly blood counts. This study was just one of many tasks that Roger would have to squeeze into his work schedule as time moved along.

Next, Dr. G. requested that he attend the Saturday morning "Child Heart Clinic", which was a division of the "State Crippled Children's Program". Here Roger learned a great detail about heart sounds, and the different types of murmurs children would have after experiencing several bouts of Rheumatic Fever. It was a real eye opener for him. He was assigned the task of teaching junior medical students the ins and outs of heart murmurs; these were numerous. As a result, Roger became especially learned concerning the heart and its' many functions and sounds; he became an expert in their interpretations as to various heart murmurs and their meanings.

Later on, Dr. G. took him out to the Hattie B. Monroe Convalescent Home, which was located in Benson, a suburb of Omaha. He was to go there each Tuesday afternoon to check the children who were convalescing from their recent attack of acute Rheumatic fever. Many times, on the way back to the med center, Dr. G would stop in Benson, at a specialty cheese shop, and buy different cheeses. He would purchase some for Roger to take home. He seemed to have taken a major interest in Roger, which made him to work all the harder to justify Dr. G's trust. After awhile, Dr. G. no longer accompanied him. He was on his own. The responsibility rested heavily on his shoulders.

At Christmas time, Dr. G and his lovely and artistic wife, Margarite, invited Marylou and Roger to their house for dinner. The house was delightfully decorated and lit by many, many candles. Dr. G had taught himself to play the piano; then, the organ. After he became somewhat proficient, he took lessons on each instrument. He gave them a short concert of his acquired prowess. What a gifted person! They had a wonderful evening. It was the highlight of their resident year's social activities.

On another occasion, Dr. G took him to the Creche Home where children stayed pending the resolution of their tangled court custody cases and similar situations. Roger was to be the doctor "On Call" if any of the children or adolescents became ill and needed care. Whew! Roger seemed to thrive on this load of many separate and different types of responsibilities.

All of the volunteer pediatricians in the pediatric department took an avid interest in Roger and taught him many different practicalities. They passed on their own acquired personal acumens. He seemed to be their "Fair Haired Boy".

Dr. George K. taught him how to easily hold an otoscope when looking at an ear so that there was very little danger of injuring the ear drum if the child suddenly moved. Dr. Floyd C. cautioned him, that when examining a child's abdomen, to touch very lightly as one could learn so much more than by using the customary heavy pressure palpation. During this year, Roger learned many practical approaches for examining children and how to interpret the findings. He tucked each pearl into his own medical knowledge bank. He was having an awesome year as he was the recipient at least two years of training crowded into one by many skilled pediatricians. By working with the different pediatricians and watching their mannerisms, he acquired a great bedside manner and patient relationship.

Back home in the new apartment, Marylou was making it into a comfortable love nest on their meager budget. Whenever Roger would think of Marylou, his thoughts about her would sparkle and remind him of the taste of a rare wine. They, both, were filled to the brim with a dizzying type of love which made their pulses spike whenever they were close to each other.

Her cooking skills were not of the best as her Mother selfishly kept the kitchen to herself and didn't teach any of her daughters any culinary arts. Such is life! Roger's cast iron stomach was up to the task of eating strange foodstuffs, some of which he did not recognize from the raw ingredients which were utilized in their making. For better or worse, Marylou valiantly tried; bravely, Roger was glad to be her guinea pig. They laughed and joked over the mishaps with each other concerning some of the cooking outcomes over supper. Roger had had to prepare his own meals frequently while growing up because his Mother worked from 1:00 pm to 11:00 pm. He was able to help Marylou with a few culinary tricks. They grew closer and closer together.

Marylou was given a fail-safe recipe for chili from a friend; "For how many victims was an unknown quantity". This recipe was faithfully followed. It ended up being delicious, but there was so much left over that they ate chili every noon and night, it seemed forever. Waste was not a permitted action in their active modus operandi. Roger supplemented their meager income by donating a pint of blood about every six weeks for which he was paid $ 25. Marylou was irritated each time that he donated but admitted that the extra money did help the budget.

Dr. G. had another little project up his sleeve for Roger. One day, he showed him an infant eating and sleeping chart. He was to ask mothers with newborns if they would participate in this study which entailed having the infant staying in the room with the mother twenty-four hours per day while in the hospital. This was a prelude to the future vogue of "Lying-in" arrangements.

In return, she would log the infant's eating and sleeping patterns. In those days, most of the mothers stayed in the hospital from five to seven days or more.

New mothers jumped at this innovation. Many of the multiparous [previous pregnancies] mothers politely declined the invitation as they knew that there would be many sleepless nights when they returned home. They wanted the respite from the many hours of getting up during the night for feedings. This rooming-in arrangement was the new vogue and thoughts were rampant about it in new birth and delivery concepts. Some mothers were thrilled, and others could easily forget it.

Some of Roger's daily routine was to demonstrate to the interns and students how to perform different procedures such as doing a paracentesis [draining off abdominal fluid] on a patient which he had done many times as an intern. He taught the practical know-how on the obtaining of blood from an infant's internal and external carotid veins in the neck and from the large femoral vein in the groin area. Roger's finger skills had become very apt. He was molding into an excellent teacher following in the footsteps of Dr G. He seemed to thrive on these duties.

Roger's year was passing by very quickly. The new Childrens' Hospital was completed and about to be ready to receive patients.

CHAPTER 12
THE START OF CHILDRENS' HOSPITAL

March 1947 arrived, and Roger's job load increased one more time. Childrens' Hospital was going to be opened soon and was in the frenzied throes of preparing to admit patients. Roger helped to put IV sets together, consisting of rubber tubing, glass adapters, and glass needle holders; spinal trays; and cut down sets. Once the necessary supplies were packaged, everything needed to be autoclaved to make them safe and sterile.

Dr. Henske desired to admit the first patient to Childrens, and so it came to pass. It was a five year old boy, who would have a hernia repaired. Roger performed this first history and physical for the hospital. He would be on call for any problems at Childrens; as well as at the med center. He was a very busy person and fulfilled Dr. Henske's admonishment of, "Did he want to work". Famous last words as Roger found out. The med center assigned an intern to sleep in the hospital to handle any problems that might occur; but Roger still was the chief major domo and subject to be called if need be.

One day, Marylou thought she should call Roger about an infant who did not seem right to her. Just thinking of him made his name bloom in her own heart. She proceeded to call him from the nursery telling him about this infant which was developing a deep bronze color.

Marylou was proving to be an exceptional nurse and was promoted to be the assistant supervisor of the nursery with a nice raise in salary. Roger was so proud of her. They held a small celebration, just the two of them, which was capped off with many, many kisses and tender loving caresses when they went to bed.

Previously, Roger had been reading in the library about a new problem identified in newborn infants consisting of a rH positive infant and a rH negative mother. This was a serious problem of blood incompatibility as its aftermath usually resulted in an infant with cerebral palsy, mental retardation, and other untoward problems. He felt that this infant had this problem, and Dr. G concurred.

Dr. G and Roger hurried to the library to determine what to do and how to do it. The pediatric literature was very sparse concerning this affliction as it was so new. It only, recently, was diagnosed. This diagnosis was based upon the recent determining of some of the newer aspects of sub blood group typing, which had not been possible before.

These new articles recommended an exchange transfusion where the infant's blood was removed and exchanged with type O rH negative blood. The procedure was hazardous, at best, to the newborn.

All of these important facts were described in detail to the mother by Roger. She elected to proceed with an exchange transfusion in lieu of the alternative outcome of doing nothing.

The few articles available recommended withdrawing fifty cc of blood and replacing it with fifty cc's of the O rH negative blood alternating until the entire baby's blood had been changed. The process depended upon a dilution phenomena. A pint of O negative blood was the recommended type to be used; it was so ordered from the laboratory.

The infant was covered with a circumcision drape, which had a small hole in the middle of it. The umbilical cord was pulled through the hole creating a sterile field. The umbilical vein was located, a #18 gauge needle was inserted into this vein. Roger held the needle in place while Dr. G. pushed and pulled the blood in and out of the infant.

The large volume of blood utilized with each syringe full was too much for the infant's circulation and tiny heart to handle. The infant became more and more lethargic during the procedure and demise occurred.

From the post mortem autopsy, it was determined that the infant's brain was heavily stained with a dense yellow color indicating that there was extensive damage already in place. In addition, the infant's heart was greatly dilated from the large volumes of blood utilized. The heart was about the size of a walnut. The infant's mother was informed of the autopsy findings in great detail. She was cautioned about future pregnancies would result in the same or worse complications.

When doing future rH exchanges, Roger determined that the thirty to fifty cc's in and out of the infant were much too much for any infant's small heart and circulation to endure; and would frequently result in the death of the infant due to heart failure from overloading. Such was the end result in this case.

As a result of these findings, Roger became an avid student of the understanding of the physiology and circulation of the newborn; and developed some forward looking policies to follow if and when another situation like this current one should arise. From his studies, he resolved to use no more than ten cc's of blood at any one time either in or out of the baby. The infant's venous pressure and heart rate needed to be frequently monitored throughout the procedure. These decisions proved to be a valuable approach in his many future endeavors.

Oh! My! Roger hurt deeply whenever he lost a patient. Marylou knew how this affected him whenever he was in a deep funk over something bad. She developed several ways to help him recover his perspective as a doctor. Marylou had great compassion and conjured up a number of techniques to console him; so that he could carry on "Saving lives and stamping out disease". She was his lodestone. This philosophy of "Saving lives and stamping out disease" became his mantra for the rest of his days thanks to Marylou. It was obvious to any onlookers that they were very good for each other; just as Roger had hoped for and prayed for such a wonderful helpmate. These traits would last all through their future life together.

Roger's residency took on a big, big new task in March of 1947; his life underwent a great upheaval. Dr. G told him that he was leaving the med center to go into practice with Dr. Tompkins. The State Maternal and Child Health Program, which paid his salary - not the med center, would not guarantee him any security for his wife, Margarite; so he had no other choice but to leave. Roger was devastated.

Help! Now, Roger had to manage the Pediatric services entirely by himself. Dr. Henske still made Sunday rounds with him, but the help from any of the Volunteer Faculty was meager and few and far between. Help! Help!

There was the outpatient clinic, the ward, the nursery, ward teaching of med students, and student nurses, Childrens' Hospital, and a host of other tasks were all on his platter; he was expected to handle them. Wow! Roger rose to the occasion. He had quickly learned how to multitask and have everything come out on schedule. A trait he would use extensively in his future medical endeavors.

One day, Roger received a call from the Emergency Room Intern about a critically ill child with a high fever, and red spots on his abdomen The male child was about eight years old. He hurriedly went to the ER with a knot in his stomach and his mind rapidly recalling to mind possible causes for this problem. The intern briefed him on the patient's history and physical findings.

Roger rapidly swung into action by ordering sterile precautions to be instituted immediately; he dressed in a sterile gown complete with cap, mask, and gloves. He told that any folks who had had contact with the patient to go home as soon as possible, to shower, and to put their clothes into the laundry without fail.

With knots in his stomach and with fear and trepidations of what he would find, Roger entered the examining room. It was obvious that this child was critically ill. He did a stat [immediate] spinal tap and found a milky solution instead of the usual clear crystal fluid. As he had surmised, this boy had a case of acute Meningococcus Meningitis and was highly infective to others.

He drew blood cultures and sent different types of specimens to the laboratory. Next, he performed a "Cut Down" on the child's ankle vein for a permanent IV installation for penicillin and other ongoing needs. A million units of penicillin was given immediately per the IV. He had the nurse call the pediatric floor and to prepare the one isolation room, which was there, for the patient and to set up strict isolation techniques around the clock, pronto! The patient would soon be there.

After setting all these wheels in motion, Roger proceeded to visit with the mother concerning the child's antecedent activities, the onset, and the seriousness of this problem. There was no doubt that this case was one of Meningococcus Meningitis. He had the typical stiff neck and back, headache, malaise, semi-stupor, a red spotted rash, and a purulent spinal fluid. This was a very contagious disease and had to be handled cautiously by everyone to avoid spreading it.

Roger placed the child on a gurney and personally transported him to the isolation room in pediatrics. His next task entailed writing the detailed medical orders for the treatment, fluids, and nutrition of the child. He ordered that the ER particular examining room be closed and sanitized before being used again. It was done.

Roger's stomach was in a knot, and was filled with multiple anxieties. He felt so alone without any expert help. He picked up the phone and called Dr. G at his office. When his voice came on the phone, Roger immediately felt better. He explained his delimina and reviewed what had been done. Dr. G reassured him that everything was under control and to continue this regime for a full ten days; then, repeat the spinal fluid examination and cultures.

It was touch and go for several days before the child began to turn the corner towards recovery. Every time Roger had to examine the child, he would have butterflies in his stomach worrying about his own possible exposure or the possibility of bringing of the disease home to his wonderful Marylou. Fortunately, all went well. Roger began to comprehend that pediatrics could be dangerous and be a major health hazard to himself and others at times.

Behind his back, Roger's stock went way up with all of the hospital personnel as the fine beginning of a pediatrician. Marylou basked in the wake of this adulation. He was her man!

In late June 1947, he received notice from the Surgeon's Office to report in uniform as a First Lieutenant to the Brook Army Medical Center in San Antonio, Texas for his basic training as a US Army Medical office. He began to make the necessary plans to report as ordered.

Roger reviewed his past year of residency, he noted that he had cared for infants, children, and adolescents with many different illnesses, and the same age brackets of healthy infants, children, and adolescents regarding how they grew and developed. It had been a most unusual residency experience with the crowding of at least two or three years of training into this one year. He was so grateful that he elected to stay at the med center. The frosting on his cake and dessert was the wonderful marriage he had with Marylou. My! What a year! He thanked his lucky stars many times over and the good Lord for Marylou, who had helped him through thick and thin.

PART 3

ROGER KING M.D. US ARMY MEDICAL CORPS

LIEUTENANT ROGER KING M.D. USMC

CHAPTER 13

BROOKE ARMY MEDICAL TRAINING CENTER AND BEYOND

Roger studied which route would be the most economical and feasible method to travel to San Antonio, Texas. He enjoyed showing his precious Marylou new experiences and adventures as she had never been outside the State of Nebraska.

Finally, he determined that the Missouri-Pacific Railroad would meet all of their needs; and so it came to pass. In addition, he made a reservation at the historic Menger Hotel for the first few nights that they would be in San Antonio, and a long term arrangement was made with a Motel Unit near the Brooks Army Medical Training Center.

With his Mother's financial aid of a loan for his uniform, Roger was outfitted with his required items of an officer's blouse, pink trousers, and billed cap until he learned what else would be needed. They decided to travel light having no means of transportation when they arrived in San Antonio. They packed the barest of essentials.

The train ride was long and wearing as they traveled coach and had to sit up two days and nights. They were glad to arrive, shower, and put on a change of clothes. They ate supper at the Menger Hotel on the beautiful outdoor dining patio; then, went straight to bed to await another day.

As they had a whole day available before reporting to the Center, they located their motel and moved in. After being settled, they were relaxing and enjoying some leisure time on the lovely lawn in front of their unit, when who should come moseying along, but his old classmate Johnny Brown and his lovely wife, Dorothy. What an amazing coincidence!

The Browns had driven from Omaha. John offered a ride to Roger to go to the Brooke Army Medical Center the next morning. Previously, Johnny had scoped out the best way to get there and knew where to report. What a welcome relief this news was. Morning came; they reported to the Adjutant Officer; received their first paycheck; and detailed instructions on their training program, which they studied intently.

They must report each morning without fail at 7:00 am for roll call and calisthenics. Ugh! Everyone in their incoming group was so out of shape that the morning exercises were an hour of sheer torture. Classes, classes, classes and more classes were the name of the game from 8:00 am to near 5:00 pm Monday through Friday when "Retreat" occurred with the lowering of the flag. The subjects had been about everything conceivable and imaginable.

The wives were invited to attend the sessions on meat procurement, processing, and selection. This was a very enlightening class. In addition, the potential medical officers were instructed in the art and skills of food handling, sanitation, and safety. These classes were very practical and interesting. After "Retreat" on Fridays, they were free until Monday. It was a thrilling ceremony for Roger to watch the Flag to be slowly lowered.

General health was discussed relating to living in a barracks, the reasons for the requirement of sleeping head to foot, which assisted in avoiding airborne diseases, were enumerated. These requirements were greatly emphasized as was body cleanliness and hygiene.

The many talks and films on venereal disease turned Roger's stomach as they were so explicit and graphic. Ugh! Are these talks necessary? As time passed, he learned that they were and then some. Another big Ugh! What a sordid experience these films were!

The days ended about 4:30 pm, then home for a relaxing change of pace. Marylou was like a breath of fresh air when he arrived at their unit. Many times during a romantic evening with the twinkling stars overhead, they would make passionate love Texas style and share their innermost thoughts. Their time in Texas was similar to finally having their long delayed honeymoon. When their lips would meet in a tasty kiss, the stars seemed to explode; they became lost in each other. They knew they would have a lifetime of tomorrows together. Marylou was so glad that she accepted the moon and the stars which her husband had offered her when they were courting. He was completely and utterly hers; she belonged to him; how could there be such a wonder?

As a matter for the record, they lost themselves in each other and slowly and deliciously moved from the teenage designated "Second Base" to a winning "Home Run" with all of its passion and pleasant aftershocks included. Oh my!

Roger thought that Marylou had great legs especially when she wore high heels. She possessed such a confident stride when walking. Yum! Yum! His mouth would water just thinking about what a tasty treat she was

They were free on the weekends and joined many excursions with the Browns. Austin, Texas was one such destination. They went through an oil exploring and producing exhibit in the University of Texas Museum. This display was fabulous and very educational. They visited the State Capital building and joined a tour which ended with a climb up many narrow steps to the dome of the building. This was a harrowing climb because the very winding metal stairway was only wide enough for one. There could be not any passing of one past another going up or down.

As they climbed up, up, and up even higher, it was like a climb to the stars. Folks were cautioned NOT to look down. Some silly person ahead did, experienced extreme height fright, immediately froze in place, and could not move another step either up or down. All on the stairs were stuck where they were. There was no place to turn around or bypass one another; everyone had to back down one step at a time all the way to the floor. Neither the Browns nor the Kings elected to try the climb again and moved on to their next encounter.

They returned home exhausted from this busy day. Their next weekend trip was to view the Gulf of Mexico and the City of Corpus Christi. This weekend came and with it another adventure was encountered. It was about a three hour drive to Corpus Christi. They had to cross a long causeway enroute. They arrived in the late morning, obtained motel units, had lunch, and decided to try some Gulf fishing.

Off they went, found a tourist fishing vessel, boarded it, and proceeded to sea. The ship personnel held a fishing contest for the passengers to see who would catch the biggest fish. Miracles of miracle, Marylou caught a large "Drum" fish and won the contest. She had never fished before. Their friends were shocked at her prowess.

Poor old John! Was he ever seasick! He sat in the stern of the boat, holding his head, and hanging over the railing when his stomach rebelled again and again. As soon as they returned to port and dry land, he miraculously recovered. They decided to cool off with a dip in the ocean. It was about 4:00 pm, and no one cautioned them about the jelly fish.

While cavorting in the delightful warm waters, they noticed a number of floating jelly fish drifting towards shore with the incoming tide. They were in the jelly fishes' pathway and began to feel stings on arms, legs, and trunk. With howls of pain, they dashed for the shore and quickly left the waters as it now was teaming with these floating hellions. Enough is enough! Why didn't someone warn them!

After a shower and change of clothes, it was time for dinner. They found a lovely restaurant. It featured "Pecan Pie" which neither Marylou nor Roger had ever heard of or had tasted. Being reassured, they gave it the old college try and were pleasantly surprised at how delicious this pie was. They endeavored to eat it again and again whenever the opportunity arose.

The next morning, it was back to San Antonio and the Training Center. On their free time, Roger and Marylou would explore different aspects of San Antonio by bus. One trip took them to the beautiful Chinese Sunken Gardens which had been developed in an old stone quarry. There were many water pools and fountains in the garden with the musical bubbling of the waters singing their songs of love. There were many lily pads with rosy red, saucy yellows, and stark white blooms. It was very quiet and peaceful time. They visited these gardens many times.

On another occasion, they went to the San Antonio Zoo, which was very unique for its time. There were no cages or bars; instead, there was a wide, deep pit between the animals and the public. It was scary, at first, to look the tawny lions with their large furry manes around their necks, and the striped tigers right in their eyes. One visit was enough for them as compared to the Sunken Gardens, which beckoned them to return again and again.

They were very disappointed when they walked along the main San Antonio Plaza and stopped for a visit to the Alamo. It was so decrepit, rundown, and dirty. It certainly needed some tender loving care and upgrading.

It was delightfully romantic when they strolled around the plaza hand in hand hearing the sweet refrains from the popular song, "You Can't Be True Dear". They heard it so much everywhere they went that the music became etched in their minds like a theme song. Whenever they heard this tune in their future years, San Antonio and their special times together would quickly come to mind. These were such carefree days. Roger was amazed to discover the many different facets and abilities that Marylou possessed. Every day, there was a new adventure with her into their unexplored lands of paradise. He admired and appreciated each and every experience. It was like finding many special presents under the Christmas tree with all of the attendant excitement and enjoyment.

One day, Marylou and Dorothy Brown went to the Officer's Club to use the pool. Dorothy had previously driven John and Roger to the Training Center for the car. Suddenly, Marylou slipped on the wet concrete and fell very hard on her pretty and well rounded left "Tush". Oh! How it hurt! When Roger came home, he packed her with ice to cut down on the swelling and the pain. This went on for several days; then, he changed to hot packs to help the swelling go away. Over time, things corrected themselves. Oh, how Roger hated to have Marylou be subjected to any kind of discomfort, let alone pain. It seemed to hurt him as much as it did her.

When Marylou became irritated over something, she gave Roger the "Look", which would freeze a brass monkey. In turn, Roger would call her "Mrs. Nasty Nice". Oh sweet love! In a short while, peace would reign again as neither one could remain miffed for very long; they had vowed never to go to bed angry. Most of the time that was the case; but being human, there were a few exceptions over the ensuing years.

One day, Roger walked to the local grocery store for several items including a large bottle of milk. On the way home, a flash flooding rain happened which filled the streets with curb high water. There were no storm sewers in San Antonio as the water table was too high to permit them.

The bottom of the sack got wet, became soggy, broke, and dropped the large bottle of milk cur plunk right smack dab on Roger's right great toenail. Oh, how that hurt! He emitted forcefully, "Thunder Turtles and various other epithets". He hobbled in great pain home and applied ice; later on, hot soaks. For the next week, doing the required morning calisthenics was enduring extreme discomfort. The army accepted no excuses for missing the morning routine. Shucks!

There was a brochure in the motel unit about the San Jose Mission, which was about a mile outside of town; so they decided to go there for their next excursion. They boarded the bus, which would take them to the end of the line near the Mission.

When they climbed aboard the bus, they casually moved to the back of the bus. The bus sat and sat and made no effort to move. Finally, the bus driver impatiently screamed out, "They couldn't sit back there and to move their "Posteriors" forward". He was rather uncouth; so with great embarrassment, they moved. It finally dawned on both of them that things were very different and segregated in the South, including separate bathrooms for the races. They managed to make major allowances for the differences. It seemed very strange to them. Oh well! "When in Rome do as the Romans do"!

When they reached the end of the line, a big sign told them that the Mission was a mile up the highway. Oh No that far! They debated the pro's and con's of the walk in the heat or should they bag this trip.. After due consideration, they decided to walk to the Mission; which they proceeded to do. Ugh! It was a hot, thirsty, dusty, and unpleasant walk along the highway with cars whizzing by. However, the trip turned out to have been well worth all of the discomfort.

The restored Mission was a lesson in history in and of itself. The Franciscan Monks had built this edifice. It was a self containing Monastery regarding food, water, and other essentials. The monks farmed in a limited fashion for their own needs. Marylou and Roger explored the Mission and learned much about the Monks and life at that time in history.

The Franciscan Monks had established a chain of Missions about twenty miles apart across New Mexico, Arizona, and up the coast of California to San Francisco. They remembered seeing the one in San Fran. What a feat! What a wonderful chapter for the history books. Roger was a serious history buff and loved explaining different points to

Marylou; sometimes ad nauseum to her dismay. Ha! After awhile, she just pretended to be interested in what he had to say.

At long last, their six weeks of training in San Antonio was up; and the day of duty assignments reared its uncertain head. Help! Roger couldn't believe it! The Army had him being a ship surgeon and riding the waves all over the Pacific Ocean. He rebelled big time, and went to the Appeals Board to protest his assignment. "What a waste of my pediatric training riding a ship would be. Isn't there a post with dependents and children needing me"? He asked, and then showed them his Certificate of Pediatric Training from the Omaha Medical Center in Pediatrics. His residency was so new that it had not been listed in the official certified residency catalog. At long last and after much haggling, Roger was exonerated and reassigned to Governour's Island and the First Army Headquarters. This island was off the tip of Manhatten in New York City. Whew! What a relief and close call!

They planned, with a certain amount of sadness, to leave the fleecy white clouds and the azure blue skies behind in Texas along with the Browns. Roger and Marylou often had close encounters of the most intimate nature, and made loving each other a study in passion. These days were so carefree from any major responsibilities after their hectic year at the Omaha Med Center; it was like being in their own heavenly universe. But like all good things, it had to come to an end, and so it did.

CHAPTER 14

A DAY IN CHICAGO AND NIAGRA FALLS

New York was a long, long way from San Antonio. Roger studied and studied the possible routes to travel in order to see as much of the countryside and sights as were available. This amount of travel was all brand new to his loved one. He was bound and determined to show her as much interesting countryside as possible. He had been to Chicago in 1933 when he was ten years old to see the World's Fair and had traveled with his Mother and sisters through the East. He remembered much about this trip.

They decided on taking the Missouri Pacific Railroad, once again, and traveled to Chicago. They arrived during the morning hours; found a nice place to eat breakfast; set out to enjoy a new group of adventures. He loved watching her beautiful brown eyes become huge with new scenes. Truly, Roger was so totally smitten with Marylou and that she was his lodestone, guiding star, and would remain so forever after.

After breakfast, they walked along Lake Michigan to the Shedd Aquarium as their first stop. It was fascinating seeing the large number of different fish from minnows to sharks from all over the world. Satiated seeing the various fish sights, they wandered past the famous Buckingham Fountain which was a Chicago landmark. Later, they ventured into the Field Museum of Natural History. All of these places were clustered nearby within walking distance. Once again, the museum was an exciting place to browse and learn. Roger enjoyed it much more than Marylou.

They spent several hours perusing the halls and exhibits of the museum which seemed endless. In a nearby park, they saw one of the statues that Dr. G's wife's, Margarite, father had sculpt. He was an internationally noted sculptor.

They walked hand in hand along Michigan Avenue, browsed windows, and dreamed while looking at the exclusive, expensive, and elegant boutiques and fashion stores. It was enjoyable to amble along and just ponder "Some Day".

After lunch, they again strolled along the shores of Lake Michigan which seemed as big as an ocean to them. They visited the elongated Navy Pier, which protruded into Lake Michigan, and was a major land mark. This entire area that they been exploring was the previous site of the 1933 Chicago World's Fair.

Alas, tempus flugit, and it was time to go across town to the New York Central Train Station. Upon arrival, they checked in for the night train to Niagra falls which traveled through Canada. The ticket agent told them for an extra $5.00 they could have a lower bunk as this train had sleeper cars. This convenience they purchased. After boarding and getting ready for bed, they snuggled and cuddled sweetly wrapped in each other's arms in the narrow bunk – whispering sweet nothings in each other's ears and listening to the musical songs of the train wheels until they were pleasantly relaxed and sung to asleep.

Marylou began to suspect that the romantic trysts they had under the Texas stars with the soft, quiet nights had accomplished its purpose, she was fairly sure that she was pregnant! She gloried in this state and kept this secret to herself. When she was certain, she told Roger; then they both reveled in the joy, and thanked the good Lord for their coming blessed event.

They arrived at Niagra Falls, had breakfast, and started exploring. There were several museums to visit, some of which had evidence of past silly and fruitless attempts to go over the Falls in rubber balls, barrels, and similar crazy stunts.

Taking a tour, they took the elevator to beneath the American Falls where they were given heavy rain gear including rain hats. This tour took them along board walks to an area just below the Falls. The water roar was so loud one could not talk and be heard. The noise and force of the Falls was awesome and somewhat frightening due to the overwhelming power of the water cascading into the river below.

There was a boat, "The Maid of the Mist", which went right into the heart of the misty waters and ventured close to the base of the Falls. Roger and Marylou were not interested. They had had enough mist from the board walk tour.

As it grew towards dusk, they wandered over the "Rainbow Bridge" to the Canadian side of the Falls where they found a quaint romantic place to eat supper and waited for darkness to descend. When it was deemed dark enough, there was a spectacular colored light show which played on both the America and Canadian Falls. This show was mind boggling to both Marylou and Roger. They had never seen its like!

When the show was over, they wandered back to the Train Depot and learned that they still had their bunk available for the trip to Albany, New York. Boarding, they sped on towards their next adventure glorying in their good fortunes of being able to be together and not being separated by oceans.

CHAPTER 15

NEW YORK CITY AND GOVENOURS ISLAND

Upon arriving at the Albany, New York Train Depot, having breakfast was the first item on their agenda. The next step on their odyssey to New York City was to locate the Hudson River Day Line, "The River Queen". Ah Ha! There she was! It was time to board and sail away over the horizons.

The day was spent slowly meandering down the river past many historic places located along the banks. The vessel was a stern wheeler and kicked up a layer of spume as it fought against the early morning incoming ocean tide surging up the river.

The foam, which was spewed out by the drive wheel of the boat, floated majestically on the ripples caused by this massive wheel until they were evaporated by the sun. Many flecks of foam crowded together to form a raft and traveled along after the passage of the vessel. As the miles passed bye, Roger and Marylou were enthralled with the scenic riverside and the various towns they passed. As they watched, the river sparkled like having so many scattered jewels reflecting the dancing sunlight beams.

Roger was the consummate history buff and enjoyed explaining the various sites that they passed. The Hudson River was first explored by the Dutch sailor, Henry Hudson, for whom the river is named. Roger had such a pleasant and interesting way of explaining history that listeners could close their eyes and visualize what he was relating. Nearby passengers inched closer and closer to listen to him.

They obtained lunch from the vessel's snack bar consisting of a sandwich and a can of soda. As they traveled along, Roger painted word pictures of how the fur trappers, clothed in their fringed deerskin outfits and coonskin caps, would come down the Hudson in the spring with their canoes piled high with prime pelts on the way to trading posts. Their paddles would flash in the sun with water drops flying off of the paddles creating a myriad of rainbows and sparkling diamonds as their canoe traveled onward. The closer the Trading Post was located to New York City the better the prices they received for their wares.

New York City was becoming a major commercial city much because of the Erie Canal,[3] which extended from the City of Buffalo on Lake Erie to Albany, New York on the Hudson. The canal was built in 1825 and was 363 miles long. It was quite an engineering feat in those early days. This canal provided for the easy transport of grain and other materials from the Midwest to the East, especially, Ohio Valley grain. This waterway helped New York City become the Chief US Shipping Port. This canal created a man-made waterway, which was the Nation's first major water transportation system.

---

[3] Erie Canal - Wikipedia

The Mohawk Indians occupied this area and were part of the Iroquois League of Indians[4]. Chief Joseph Brant was the principal leader in the French and Indian wars against the British and later in the Revolutionary War. During the French and Indian Wars, the Hudson River was the major invasion pathway for the French coming down from Canada to raid and pillage the settlers leaving chaos in their wake. Their Indian allies were ruthless in the killing and maiming of the unlucky settlers in their path.

The British used this waterway in a similar manner during the Revolutionary War. The Hudson Valley was fraught with much history and many historical places. As they journeyed along, the big stern wheel of the Day Liner created quite a wake as it bucked the ebbing tides from the ocean.

They passed Kingston which was the early capital of New York much before Albany. Poughkeepsie was nestled along the banks. It was an Old Dutch Town where Lafayette had visited, then, came Hyde Park where President Franklin Roosevelt spent much of his time when escaping from the humid rigors of Washington D.C. summers and where he is buried.

As the river wended itself along, a major point of history, then, and now came into view. There was West Point, where General Benedict Arnold[5] became such a national traitor when he plotted to put the various Forts located at the Point into the hands of the British. These forts controlled the traffic on the Hudson. He still lives in infamy as the major traitor from the Revolutionary War as he could have caused irreparable damage had he not been discovered and ousted. Unfortunately, he escaped to the British lines. He died in shame.

West Point was, and is, the site of the famous Military Academy where many important men in history were trained, and many were buried here; including the incomparable General of the Armies Douglas MacArthur. Much of the making of the early aspects of the United States centered along this Hudson River Valley corridor.

Storm King Park and Bear Mountain were lovely sights to encounter. Roger remembered them from his visit here in 1933. The current trip was so enticing and filled with many sweet memories as Roger's wonderful Marylou was beside him making his world beautiful and unforgettable. When Roger looked at Marylou, he heart was gripped with elemental and inexhaustible devotion towards her which was like the sweet taste of ambrosia.

When he told her that he loved her again and again, her heart pounded as though it was going to jump out of her chest. She began to realize how empty her life had been before she became his. Whenever he kissed her in a long and lingering manner, her breath paused just a minutia away from his lips as he whispered, "I love you". She replied, "I might get used to you saying that after a few hundred times".

Later on, the community, Croton-on-the Hudson, was passed by; then Stony Point[6] was sighted where General "Mad" Anthony Wayne fought one of the last battles of the Revolutionary War in order to obtain control of the Hudson River. White Plains was passed, and at long last, Pier 36 of New York City was reached.

---

[4] Mohawk People / Joseph Brant Wikipedia

[5] Wikipedia: Benedict Arnold - Biography

[6] Wikipedia: General Anthony Wayne

They arrived intact and ready for the next episode in their odyssey. As the boat maneuvered into its mooring slip on Pier 36, they observed the magnificent New York Skyline. Roger proceeded to the Tourist Information Booth where the helpers arranged a hotel room for them at the Tudor in lower Manhattan. The next day, he proceeded to Governour's Island and reported to the Adjutant where he received two major devastating blows:

1. There was no Guest House or Quarters on the Island
2. There were no dependents located here.

Oh Dear! What was he to do? Back he went to the Hotel where he conferred with Marylou as to the options they might take.

It was obvious, they could not remain in the hotel very long; so the first item on their agenda was to locate a place to live. This seemed like a monumental task at this moment in time and in this teeming city.

They contacted a "Real Estate Agency" in the neighborhood of the this hotel and proceeded to look at available places. They found one on 57th Street on the Westside near Central Park and the famous Plaza Hotel located on 56th street. They paid their "Finder's Fee" to the agent and moved into a one room efficiency apartment on the first floor in a Brown Stone building.

CHAPTER 16

LIVING IN NEW YORK CITY

Their apartment was small, compact, and contained a tiny kitchenette. Marylou was experiencing some morning sickness; but like the trooper she was, it was tolerated, and as much as possible did not let it stop her activities

Their neighbors were quite unusual. On the second floor lived a man who had two Great Dane dogs. He took them out for walks two or three times a day. Oh joy! On the third floor, there came a loud yodeling type of noise and over time they discerned that the noise they heard began to settle into a set of operatic scales going up and down, seemingly forever. What unusual noises and people this apartment contained. Oh well, such was life in New York City!

Roger had to board the subway each morning just a few blocks from their apartment. The first few days as he rode the subway, he noticed that many of the passengers did not speak English. There was a mixture of many tongues of passengers, who were hanging from the ceiling straps and reading their newspapers while standing up. Within the week, Roger was doing the same thing with his own paper. It was a long ride to Battery Park.

After about thirty minutes he reached the end of the line, he had to walk through and around a number of inebriated bodies lying on the ground in Battery Park. He strolled to the ferry landing for Governour's Island, boarded the vessel, and journeyed off to the Island.

When on the Island, Roger found that he had very little to do. There were no dependents and no children who needed his care. How was he going to keep busy? Doing nothing or trying to find busy work was such a grind after his med center years that it was an antithesis to Roger. He sought out the First Army Adjutant and requested a transfer to an Army Post where he would be utilized as a pediatrician. He was told consideration might be given to his request, meanwhile, he was to keep occupied. "Doing what"? he thought.

Roger spent a considerable amount of time sitting on the island seawall watching the great ocean going vessels pass by. Over time, he recognized the Queen Mary and the Queen Elizabeth plying back and forth between Southampton and New York City.

He had to take his turn at being the Medical Officer of the Day, which meant that he would staying on the Island over the weekend. Marylou would be alone. She was petrified and stayed awake with fright most of the night. She was terrified by the strange sounds that she heard coming from the street. It was awful for her being in the apartment alone in this strange city. She did not feel comfortable with the poor lock on her door; consequently, she cowered in their bed most of the night. It was sheer torture for her when this duty came to Roger, as it did every few weeks.

On the weekends, Roger and Marylou set out to explore the mysteries and sights of the City. Over time, they journeyed to the top of the Empire State Building, to the famous Bronx Zoo, Grant's Tomb, and out to the Statue of Liberty. On Sundays, they would go to Mass at St. Patrick's Cathedral, which was a magnificent edifice having a colorful celebration of pomp and ceremony. They ventured to Coney Island and were badly disappointed in how dirty and run down it was. Many of the museums were visited along with the multitude of Art Galleries, located seemingly, everywhere. Poor Roger could not find anything artistic in the popular contemporary art works and was bored stiff when this type of art was encountered.

They would window look at the famous stores like Sacs Fifth Avenue and Macy's. The Skating Rink at Rockefeller Center was fun to visit and watch the skaters with their blades flashing while doing their twirling and jump stunts. They would stop for tea at the rink level café.

After about six weeks of worry and frustration, the Adjutant called him to the office and informed him that he was to be transferred to Fort Dix, New Jersey. Oh Joy! Roger could hardly wait to go home and tell Marylou of their good fortune.

Part 4

Life at Fort Dix and Brown's Mills

CHAPTER 17

FORT DIX

They quickly packed their few belongings and headed for the train station, booked seats to Bordentown, New Jersey, which was close to the Fort. They were grateful to see the blue sky and acres of green grass without having to travel blocks and blocks or acquire a sore neck from craning upward to obtain a glimpse of the sky.

They arrived at Bordentown; sought a place to stay, and located a clean, quiet, rooming house with one room available, which they rented. No food was allowed in the rooms; so they ventured three times a day to the nearby Highway Diner and the town's only bona fide restaurant. The food was very good. The selections were not too bad. After awhile, they knew the menus by heart. They enjoyed the jute box music which frequently played Perry Como singing, "Cool Clear Water" over and over again until the song became etched in their minds.

The owners of the rooming house, Mr. and Mrs. Johns took a liking to Marylou and had pity on her morning sickness. Mrs. Johns allowed her to keep some crackers in their room. Sometimes, it was difficult for her control the queasiness and still go out for breakfast.

On several Sundays, the owners suggested that Roger and Marylou go for a ride with them to see the countryside, which they did. Though Roger was only a Lieutenant, Mr. Johns always called him, "Captain", much to his chagrin.

Roger took the bus to Fort Dix and reported to the Post Surgeon's office where he met several members of the medical staff. There were no quarters on the Post. He was informed that it would be about a month before the current post pediatrician, John Allen, would be discharged. John offered to speak with his landlord about renting Roger his house, which was located about five miles from the fort in a resort area called Brown's Mills. The owner agreed to the rental, and was happy to have Roger as a tenant.

The owner was a doctor in Philadelphia and previously used this cabin in the pines for a summer retreat; but no longer was it useful to him as his family had grown and left his feathered nest. He rented it for the income and maintenance costs.

Roger was destined to care for the dependents' children; another physician, Elmer Mueller an Internist, would care for the dependent wives.

There was a Sergeant Smith and his wife from Wooster, Massachusetts who lived at the boarding house and wanted to sell their used Chevrolete coupe for $300. While Roger was at the Fort, Marylou went to the bank, using Roger's army insurance as collateral, borrowed the money to buy the car; which they accomplished.

The month passed quickly, and soon it was time to move into the little cabin in the pines on the edge of a national forest. Just a short distance from the house, there was a dammed up idyllic lake with a dock and bench made for daydreaming. Their little house was friendly, cozy and nestled back from the road. Frequently, they would walk hand in hand to the lake and sit on the bench on the dock. They would watch the breezes ripple the water surface and talk about their lives and future together and when their time in the service was over.

They were so in love with love and each other. Roger was conscious of Marylou, who was soft and cuddly and a very controlled woman, who liked to make her own decisions after considering all facets of a situation. This particular facet of her he learned the hard way. He greatly admired her.

He wanted her as much as she wanted him. Passion began to exploded whenever they kissed, she would feel the earth tilt. Marylou seemed to have a bottomless well of patience for adjusting to whatever she had to confront.

Roger fanned his desire for her into a consuming fire, as if was possible to love her any more than he already did. He wondered much as he stroked the soft curves of her feminine body and pondered his good fortune. There were times that he was so filled with feelings for her that he thought that his heart would swell outside of his chest or fragment into tiny pieces.

Sometimes at night, Roger would gaze out the windows at a massive sprinkling of stars and would listen to Marylou's soft, steady, and sighing type of breathing and would think how much he loved her and dreamed of their future life together.

Roger took Marylou's hand as they entered into their cabin and began to plan for their coming stork arrival in April. Marylou, in a period of introspection, reflected on Roger as the person she had married for evermore. She liked who he was, how he thought, and especially, how he listened when people were talking. He exuded politeness, strength, good common sense, compassion, and safety; she felt so protected, wanted, cared for, and desired. Frequently, she went to sleep at night with a satisfied smile on her face and had pleasant dreams concerning her life with Roger. At times, she would emit a great sigh and snuggle closer to him.

One of the first needs on Roger's agenda was to find good obstetrical care for Marylou; he traveled to Trenton, New Jersey to the Women's Hospital where he sought out the hospital administrator. He did not desire having Marylou in the care of on army obstetrician, as most of them had no more training than he had had. He wanted the best available for his wonderful Marylou.

After their detailed conversations, the administrator gave him the name of Dr. Press, the Chief of the Obstetrical Staff, as her first choice. Roger went to his office, felt comfortable with him, and made arrangements for Marylou's care. On her first visit, he received an "A+" by Marylou. She felt satisfied with the choice of Dr. Press. They made monthly trips to Trenton which was about twenty-five miles from their cabin in Brown's Mills. For her prescriptions, they drove to Pemberton, New Jersey, which was about five miles from their home to the only pharmacy in the region.. On one trip to Trenton, they purchased several maternity dresses and a pair of comfortable shoes with sturdy heels. Factitiously, Roger called them her "Mother Hubbard Shoes". This connotation did not please Marylou, and she let him know that fact.

Collectively, they decided to put Marylou's nursing career on hold until they were done with the Armed Services. With the new baby coming, it would pose many difficulties which they did not need.

Meanwhile, Roger was busy seeing children from Fort Dix, Maguire Airbase, which was close by, as was a major army general hospital. Army personnel, learned that there was a personable and competent pediatrician available so many dependents began to seek Roger for their care. Lo and behold, naval dependents even came from Lakehurst Naval Air Base where the Hindenburg Dirigible Disaster[7] had crashed and burned. He quickly became busy and loved every minute. He held a "Sick Call" each morning, first come first served, and held an afternoon "Well Baby Clinic" by appointment only. He was in seventh heaven with his work and applied so many facets to his "practice" which he had learned from Dr. G and Dr. Tompkins.

Over time, he heard about pediatric conferences in Philadelphia. With the Post Surgeon's permission, he drove there, every other Tuesday, to St. Christopher's Children Hospital in the mornings and listened to Dr. Waldo Nelson present interesting cases to his students. Dr Nelson was the author of the universally used pediatric textbook, "Nelson Textbook of Pediatrics". In the afternoon, Roger traveled across town to Philadelphia's Children's Hospital where he listened to Dr. Joseph Stokes present cases to his medical students. Dr. Stokes was well known and highly respected as one of the top pediatricians in the country. Such opportunities to enhance Roger's thirst for knowledge were not always so readily available to everyone. He wanted to exploit any available opportunities to learn from these two outstanding men. In his mind, they complimented his Omaha mentors. Roger was what some folks might disparagingly call an "Eager Beaver".

Meanwhile, back home in their cabin, Marylou was making it into a love nest and preparing for their firstborn. The Trenton Sears Store had an acceptable changing table, and a bassinette which they purchased among other things such as baby clothes, diapers, and many additional essential items. They were having wonderful thoughts and dreams about their coming, "Blessed Event".

Marylou's older sister was going to be married and wanted Marylou to be her Matron of Honor; so she planned to fly home for the month of October. Oh how lonesome Roger felt day after day while she was gone. He not only counted the weeks, but the days, and even some hours until she would return. He wrote her a daily letter and kept her replies under his pillow at night after he had reread all of them, one at a time before going to sleep.

Roger casually mentioned to the Master Sergeant, who managed his clinic, that he would like to buy the popular, short, and sporty Army Eisenhower Jacket and inquired, "Where would he might go to find one"? Lo and behold a few days later, a jacket just happened to appear on his desk in his size. What a major coincidence! Roger knew better than to say, "Thank you" for fear of getting someone into trouble. He gladly wore it in the place of his officer's blouse. He was beginning to learn how the Services really operated, and who knew the keys to obtain desired materials or items. His clinic workers – service and nursing personnel, thought very highly of Roger after working with him for awhile. He was so considerate of their feelings and assistance.

As part of Roger's pediatric care, he instituted a series of "Well Child Talks" similar to those that Dr. Tompkins gave back in Omaha. They were received with great success and attendance. Colonel Threadgill, the Post Surgeon, was very pleased and happy with

---

[7] Hindenburg Disaster Wikipedia

Roger's actions and zeal. He had not received any complaints about his care, but had enjoyed receiving many accolades. This lack of complaints was rather unusual in the service.

Marylou and Roger made good use of their car traveling all around Central New Jersey. They drove to and walked around the beautiful Princeton Campus. The Battle of Princeton[8] led to the British evacuation of southern New Jersey. The university campus was located fairly close to the Shore and the Atlantic Ocean. They so liked observing the staid old buildings. Roger was very conscious of the magic that existed in Marylou's hand as they walked along.

While looking at the ocean, Marylou couldn't get over how massive the water expanse was; there was no end in sight. They drove along the coast and admired the many beach homes. Most of these homes were closed and boarded up for the winter.

Their favorite drive was to go up the Jersey side of the Delaware River to the Delaware Water Gap, then, down the Pennsylvania side to Washington's Crossing[9] of the Delaware River near Trenton and back home. They enjoyed this drive several times, stopping at a quaint restaurant about half way home called, "The Cat and the Fiddle". It was romantically situated overlooking the River. It was a delightful place to eat and were served excellent food.

Christmas time arrived; so they went into the forest, found the tree of their dreams, cut it down, and hauled it home to their cabin. It was a memorable occasion for both of them. The tree was about five feet tall and smelled so pungently of balsam odors. Its fragrance filled their little cabin creating a sweet festive air. Now, all the tree needed was some lights and decorations to complete their fairy land atmosphere. This meant that a trip to Philadelphia was in order.

Marylou loved decorating the tree after the obtaining some of these items after their trip to Philadelphia. Roger quickly learned to do whatever she told him. She was the "Boss"; Roger loved catering to her whims and desires. He fell more in love with her each day. His heart was filled with overflowing love. One morning, a Christmas snow arrived, and everywhere one looked there was a beautiful pristine fairyland. Roger worried about the roads until he looked out the window and saw that they already had been plowed.

They went to Philadelphia to do their Christmas shopping. They shopped at the big "Gimbals Store", which size was amazing to them. It was filled with Christmas décor of all types and descriptions with many red and green colors everywhere they gazed.

The Salvation Army bells were tinkling on every corner of the downtown area. They were enthralled and stimulated by all the sounds and sights of the Christmas season. Everywhere they went, Carols were heard creating the feeling of giving. People were hurrying here and there; everyone was looking like a pack mule loaded down with gift packages for their loved ones. The crowds of folks seemed so cherry and filled with the Christmas spirit. It was a glorious day for them to recount many times over when they arrived back home.

For the first time, they rode an escalator at Gimbals. Oh my! What a contrast, convenience, and difference from waiting for a crowded elevator. They found inexpensive presents for Marylou's family, a string of tree lights, a few special ornaments, and a box

---

[8] Battle of Princeton - Wikipedia

[9] Washington's Crossing of the Delaware - Wikipedia

of tinsel for their tree on their meager budget. They were so happy and were filled to the brim with the season's atmosphere. They had never, before, seen the likes of it.

Due to the luck of the draw, Roger drew Officer of the Day for New Year's Eve, and what a mess that was. Most of his night was spent, without sleep, doing sobriety checks on military personnel, who were brought in by the MP's [Military Police]. What a nauseating experience this was.

In addition, he had to check the health of the prisoners held in solitary confinement in the Guard House [jail]. They were only allowed one full meal every three days; the rest of the meals consisted of bread and water only. These tasks exposed him to the seamy side of military life and left unsavory and lasting impressions on Roger.

Many times, Roger was confronted with questions from his non-Catholic peers about abortion, church dogma, and other religious inquiries. Thanks to Father Noonan and Creighton night school, when he was a student at the med center, he could hold his own, and then some.

On another trip to Philly, the "City of Brotherly Love", they explored Independence Hall where the Constitution was proposed, cussed, discussed, and hammered into reality. They visited the big Liberty Bell and experienced the many anxieties that our founding fathers must have endured. Roger and Marylou were living in the midst of history and enjoying all facets of it. They must have encountered a million places where George Washington had slept. Ha!

The first snow fall was a wet and heavy one which added a further festive air to their tiny cabin in the woods. Deer came out of the forest and walked around their cabin uninhibited and undaunted by man or beast. The snow and deer created such a wonderful idyllic and holiday setting which they thoroughly enjoyed while snuggled and cuddled in their little dream oasis while the winter winds blew and howled. They couldn't be happier. The cabin was toasty warm due to a large propane heater. At night, the skies were a deep indigo blue and were covered with a million stars when they came out; thus creating a star spangled sky. Obviously, they loved where they lived.

They faithfully made their monthly and uneventful prenatal visits to Trenton. Thank heavens no complications were foreseen. They were so happy, and time seemed to be flying by so very fast. Marylou's pregnancy was going along without any worries or concerns, other than the usual ones most mothers experienced. Roger enjoyed listening to the beating heart of their little one, rubbing her tummy with cocoa butter to help avoid stretch marks, and to feel the baby kick his hand. He was a very active infant. Being aware of this new life was a miraculous sensation.

She began to waddle very gracefully and looked very Madonna like. Roger lost his breath whenever he looked at her as she was so beautiful in her pregnancy. He daily thanked the Good Lord for his many blessings. They would go Mass at a small mission church, St. Ann's in the Pines. The little church was lovely, nestled in the woods, and very conducive to spiritual thoughts. Father Kane was the itinerate pastor as he had a main parish elsewhere. He was very friendly, and they liked him a lot.

The fall meeting of the America Academy of Pediatrics was held in Atlantic City that year; so with permission from Colonel Threadgill, they drove there one day. They had great fun browsing the different medical and commercial exhibits. They saw some of the first paper diapers on the market, and some special nursing bottles with rubber caps, which seemed to be made for traveling..

Marylou planned to breast feed. They were amazed and somewhat overwhelmed by the size and scope of this Atlantic Meeting. They wondered, "Would they ever participate in meetings like this one"? Little did they know what their future would hold.

Time was fleeing, and the time for Marylou's delivery was fast approaching. Her Mother planned to come for the month close to when she was due to deliver. Roger and Marylou drove to Philadelphia to pick her up at the airport. Roger hated the various highway "Round-abouts" which frequented the many New Jersey Highways and Turnpikes.

The first time he encountered a roundabout, he was caught on the inside lane of the "Round" and had a devil of a time, due to the heavy traffic, edging his way to the outside lane in order to make the appropriate exit. On several occasions, he had to make several circles around before he was able to exit. "Live and Learn"! Whew what a harrowing experience! Roger soon learned how to negotiate these highway traps as they frequently went to Mount Holly for grocery shopping. This store was a forerunner of the modern supermarket.

Marylou's Mother arrived. Her airplane flight was so uneventful that she almost forgot to disembark in Philadelphia as she was so enjoying the ride. She happened to look out her window, saw Marylou, and remembered that it was time to get off. It was good to see her. Roger was greatly relieved that she came to be with them. It greatly worried him while he was at the Post working, and Marylou was home alone without a phone in case of need. At that time, a phone was almost impossible to obtain.

Mother Eva quickly took things into her capable hands; Roger's many worries and anxieties melted away like snow with a warm sun. Time quickly passed. There were soft friendly breezes whisking in from the southwest to contest the control of the atmosphere with the cold winds sailing in from the Atlantic Ocean. The tree leaf buds were beginning to spring open producing a soft, green haze to the forest. Everywhere, the land was awakening once again from its winter's deep sleep and was endeavoring to crush out the last throes of winter.

With the arrival of spring, they enjoyed walking hand and hand to the lake where they sat on the dock bench and watched the breezes ripple the waters. It was such a wonderful feeling. Roger felt that there was no way that he could be more in love with Marylou until tomorrow came when he felt his love grow even stronger. Having their firstborn was the crowning touch to their Shangri La.

On this one bright day, with the sun peeking its saucy head through the pink tainted clouds and the birds filling the air with their different symphonies of melodious songs as they happily built their nests, Marylou's water broke and contractions started. She was on time as it was mid April.

Marylou's time had arrived. Roger was beside himself as they were so far away from Trenton. Inherently, he knew the situation was much too early to leave; but off they went, anyway, to the Women's Hospital. He didn't trust his car or the distance.

She was admitted, settled down in the Maturity Ward; and, then, her contractions stopped dead in their tracks. OH No! Now what? A trip back home? Ugh! Because of the distance, her obstetrician, Dr. Press, suggested that an induction of labor be tried ; to which Roger heartily agreed; so it was started with a mild modicum of success initially.

Roger wanted to be with Marylou during her labor. No dice! There was a large Amazon, hefty, big bosomed, type of a nurse guarding the passageway to the Labor and

Delivery Suite. She reminded Roger of a bouncer or a huge Sumo Japanese wrestler. All of Roger's pleas fell on her deaf ears; and so Eva and he were relegated to the waiting area up on the fourth floor.

Time crawled along one hour, then, four, then, many more until it was almost midnight. They had gone for a bite to eat and returned to wait some more. Finally, Marylou's labor picked up; she delivered a beautiful little boy near midnight. They had decided to name him, Bobby after Marylou's Brother-in-law. Eva and Roger were ecstatic. They called everyone back in Omaha, and, then, slowly drove home filled with thankfulness that there were no apparent problems. Truly their baby was "Love made visible".

They returned to the hospital every day. Marylou wanted to nurse her baby; she tried, but due to inverted nipples it became an impossible ordeal even with nipple shields and pumping. The bottles were resorted to and instituted forthwith without any apparent problems. It was amazing to Roger, from his past experiences when mothers were kept in bed for days, that the nurses had her up and walking the next day and everyday thereafter. Obviously, this was the new philosophy in maternity scenes.

It was a glorious day for Roger when it was time to take his family home. He couldn't believe his good fortune. He had a great sense of protectiveness of his family. He loved Marylou more than anything and thought that she was a great "dish". There was such magic in her hands. Such beautiful music was played in his heart whenever he held her hand; that was all the encouragement that he needed to address their unknown future without any qualms or concerns. He couldn't have a better helpmate and soulmate.

Oops! They discovered there was no way to wash Bobby's diapers; so off to the store went Roger. After looking high and low, he found a portable counter- top washer made for small apartments. He quickly purchased the same and started the search for the nifty bottles and paper diapers they saw at the Meeting in Atlantic City. Ah Ha! Found! He bought a moderate supply. Now, there has to be a sterilizer somewhere. He searched and found what they needed; back home traveled this smug explorer. Peace reigned once more! Oh Joy! "He was her hero", so said Marylou.

Marylou's Mother had four girls and no boys. One day, she was in the bedroom changing Bobby's diaper, when a wild shriek was heard, she emerged with urine dripping from her glasses and face. Oh Dear me! With little boys, one needs to be alert and ready for a quick covering action.

Marylou's Mother journeyed home after a few weeks of helping them get settled in with their newcomer. As wonderful as she was and so helpful, there was almost no privacy; peace began to reign once more. At long last, they were alone with their baby. They were very grateful for her help, but it was time to be by themselves and to make their own mistakes in child care without any censoring eyes around.

Bobby was baptized in the little church, St. Ann's in the Pines, by Father Kane. At end of each day, Roger and Marylou would exchange little tidbits of experiences and thoughts that they had encountered during the time they were apart. It was their highlight for the day and became an ongoing habit which they relished during the ensuing years.

Marylou loved the rock solid aura Roger projected and realized how much she needed him and relied upon his judgments. Once again he made her feel safe and secure. When she drifted off to sleep at night, she portrayed a sweet smile of complete contentment.

When he told her that he loved her again and again, her heart pounded like it was going to jump out of her chest.

They were so happy in their idyllic world without a care in sight when all of a sudden their dreams were shattered and rudely disrupted. Like a bolt out of the blue, disaster destroyed their cozy world with a letter from the Surgeon General's Office ordering Roger to proceed to Sendai, Japan. "Where in God's name is that place"? thought Roger. Oh No! It can't be, that has to be at the end of the world. It was an order without any questions allowed, and had to be obeyed.

He quickly learned that when you are overseas, one had to accumulate points and wait almost a year before dependents would be authorized to join their spouses. Oh No! How could he stand being separated for a whole year from Marylou and Bobby. He would miss all of Bobby's early growth and development milestones, the changing of his diapers, and the feeding him at 2:00 am. Roger was almost beside himself.

When Roger was feeding Bobby at 2:00 am, he would say to himself, "How will I be able to stand not seeing you for a whole year". Their world had been viciously upset, shattered, and devastated.

Previously, they had encountered a problem with Bobby's formula; he would break out from the cow's milk and developed an eczema on his face which was only cleared by shifting to a special amino acid hydrolysate {Nutramigen} which was expensive and hard to obtain. Roger purchased all of this formula found in the surrounding area.

Colonel Threadgill, the Post Surgeon, did not want Roger to be transferred as he was the best pediatrician that he had ever had and had received many unsolicited compliments on Roger's work and care. The American Red Cross Hardship line was used. The Army Hardship Appeal Cause, and many other avenues were tried; all to no avail. They even tried for a special medical hardship case due to Bobby's eczema; but no dice.

They had decided, once again, that for the foreseeable future, Marylou would put her nursing career on hold until they could examine their needs and what they wanted to do when out of the service and when Roger's training was completed.

PART 5
DESTINATION YOKOHAMA
CAPTAIN ROGER KING M.D. USAC

CHAPTER 18

TAKING THE MILK ROUTE TO YOKOHAMA

Roger, having tried all of his avenues for deferment at his disposal to obtain a change in his orders and having reconciled himself to the inevitable, all of a sudden and out of the blue, a new set of orders came from the Surgeon General's Office ordering Roger and his family to proceed by coordinated travel to Japan. The orders stated that because he was a pediatrician, he could administer to his own child whenever necessary.

What an awesome responsibility that order was. They would travel by "Coordinated Travel" [meaning going together as a unit] as stated on their telegram orders. Thank heavens, they had a watchful and helpful guardian angel looking after them.

Because of all of the moves and changes, young Bobby was not too cooperative with his eating and sleeping habits. However, he was not at all embarrassed when his diaper was changed on planes, trains, and buses. Ha!

Camp Stoneman was the embarkation post for Service Pacific travel. The army had packed their few belongings, which they placed in storage in Omaha. They sold their old oil eating and reliable coupe; flew to Omaha, where they stayed with Roger's older sister, Fannie. There was not a separate bedroom available at Marylou's home; they slept in Fannie's attic, which was just fine with them as they were out of the way from all the commotion at Marylou's house. Her younger sister was to be married just a few days after they left for the west coast. This created a great deal of friction towards Roger and Marylou by this sister's temporary disruption of her wedding plans. It was not their fault; nor could they change the Army Orders; nor would they even try because it might jeopardize their going together.

Marylou's Mother thought that they were going to the ends of the earth to some heathen land! She was not a happy camper about this trip to be undertaken by her dear darling grandson and her daughter. Surely, if Roger had wanted to do so he could change things. Ha! Not a chance of a snowball in hell!

They flew to Denver, transferred planes, where they experienced a harrowing experience on the take-off. Just as the plane gained momentum reading for lift off a tire blew out creating havoc for the pilot, who fought to control the plane, to keep it on the runway, and bring it to a halt.

It was a herculean job to keep the plane from going off the runway and crashing; people were screaming, others were praying out loud. Marylou almost crushed Roger's hand grasping it so tight. They both held onto Bobby for dear life to keep him from being thrown around. It was a huge nightmare until the pilot was able to control the rocketing plane. It was a terrifying three or four minutes. This happenstance caused well over an hour's delay and lay-over; then, it was on to San Francisco. They had many misgivings about flying until they landed safely at the San Francisco airport where they finally could take a big sigh of relief.

They proceeded to take a bus for the sixty-five mile trip to Pittsburg, California where Camp Stoneman was located. Once again, there were no quarters available; so the small and dingy hotel in town had to suffice with a community bathroom down the hall. Not an ideal situation.

They arrived intact; Roger reported at the Post, where it was determined that all of their papers were in order – not really! Oh No! Not another snag in this very efficient Army system! Roger was scheduled to leave from San Francisco, and Marylou and Bobby were to leave from Seattle. Help! Help! With this gaff, Marylou and Roger had to readjust their thinking and planning. Back into the fray, Roger plunged once more waving his telegraph orders at anyone who would listen. He kept insisting that they were supposed to go together as written.

At long last, everything was ironed out; they would sail in ten days from the Treasure Island Marina[10], an island in San Francisco Bay, from whence the army transports sailed. Oh Joy! Marylou and Bobby wouldn't have to turn around and go back to Omaha. Their guardian angel rescued them once again and their prayers had been answered.

With a great deal of effort in handling all of their baggage and Bobby's needs and with no one to help, it was with an immense struggle that they moved with their baggage via a train and a ferry to San Fran and the Californian Hotel.

They carried a separate suitcase for Bobby's paper diapers, extra bottles, a hot plate, a sauce pan, and a few cans of Nutramigen. Wherever they landed, Bobby's routine would not be interrupted. They toted his bassinette along with everything else that they needed for him. They became very adept at setting up housekeeping for Bobby and could conveniently make his formula wherever they landed. At the Californian, they had a lovely hotel room with a private bath; it had a huge closet so Bobby was housed in it where he could enjoy the peace and quiet of his own room. He began to sleep better. This stay was quite a contrast to their Camp Stoneman venture.

Roger scoured all the drugstores in downtown Frisco for cans of Nutramigen and achieving only a modicum of success. This scarcity and Bobby's needs for Japan called for serious thought and dire action. Roger contacted the Mead Johnson Manager on the west coast; had lunch with him; the Manager told Roger, "There was no problem. We need to figure how much formula you will need for a year's stay", so they did.

They determined that one hundred pounds would suffice for the year. As the San Francisco docks were tied up on strike, the Manager had the necessary powdered formula shipped to Japan from Los Angeles on a boat ahead of Roger's departure. It was waiting in Sendai when they arrived. What a courtesy service this action was, and at NO cost to Roger. Wow! He never forgot this when he finally was in practice. Mead Johnson Products became his first choice for infants. Interesting enough, when they returned from Japan there was only ten pounds of Nutramigen left over. They had figured right!

At long last, they were assigned to the SS Buckner, which ship was to leave in ten days – July 10, 1949. On Sunday, they went to Mass at the San Fran Cathedral which was lovely, and that was the last time that they would be in Church for over a month.

---

[10] Treasure Island Marina Wikipedia

Any place they went had to be by cab; so their excursions were few and far between due to limited funds. They utilized their intervening time well. They took a Grey Line Tour of the Muir Woods, which was up the coast from San Fran. They did not have a stroller, and baby back packs were unheard of; therefore, Roger carried little Bobby in his arms for the entire time they were in the woods. Oh! Afterwards, how his arms ached from shoulder to wrists from carrying Bobby. What price fatherhood extracted.

My! How huge those red wood trees were! The giant Sequoia were magnificent and overwhelming. They had never seen the like. The giant red woods created a lovely canopy overhead; so that they could hardly see the sky; the woods were so quiet that it seemed that they were in a great outdoor cathedral.

When they exited from the forest, it was a gorgeous day. The sky was a deep blue with a few whip cream like white clouds floating idly along on gentle breezes. Roger felt so alive with Marylou by his side and little Bobby, who stole his heart again and again whenever he smiled. He felt so protective of his little family, which was so far from home and still had so much farther to go. This responsibility weighed heavily on his shoulders. He was very grateful to have the unflappable Marylou by his side. She was his anchor when facing their next day's trials and tribulations.

During the ensuing waiting interim, they took a city Grey Line Tour and saw the many features such as the "Top of the Mark", China Town with its colorful signs and native dresses, the Japanese Gardens, which were gorgeous, Knob Hill where the wealthy lived, Coit Tower, the Golden Gate Bridge, Cliff House, Seal Rock, an old Franciscan Mission which took them back to San Antonio, and finished the tour at Fisherman's Warf where they had a bite to eat.

Though it was early July, Marylou was cold due to the brisk chilly City weather as she did not have an appropriate coat; they journeyed forth to find one which they did pronto at Macy's Department Store. This coat made her nice and comfy cozy.

Roger's heart had the same and even more of a warm and comforting glow concerning Marylou and what a wonderful mother he thought she was. Her appearance and demeanor masked a razor sharp mind and a brilliant intelligence. He knew that he was a very lucky man and had won the Jackpot when he married her. They were no longer newlyweds; but, every time he kissed her, his pulse hammered and her's thundered. They seemed like a pair of giddy teenagers as they were so in love with each other. Whenever he murmured her name, she rejoiced as her love for him consumed her. She found herself responding with a totality that she never knew or imagined that she had. Roger was a dyed in the wool romantic. He would leave love notes around their living quarters for her to find whenever he was away. He marveled at her long eye lashes as a long sweep of black that seemed to weigh her eye lids down. Passion would stir his blood.

CHAPTER 19

ON THE HIGH SEAS

Soon it was time to proceed to the Treasure Island Marina and embark onto the large Cruise Ship, SS Buckner. In its previous life, this ship had been the Queen of the Pacific Cruise Lines and had plied the deep, blue waters of the Pacific Ocean from here to there and back again. Now, this ship carried dependents and troops to different parts of the Pacific Rim. Roger learned that as the ship surgeon, he was to be the third office in command of this ship just beneath the Ship's Captain and the Ship's Troop Commander. What an awesome responsibility this was. Off to sea, they ventured.

They passed under the Golden Gate Bridge, hit the Pacific rollers, and journeyed on into the vast blue Pacific Ocean. As soon as they cleared the land, there was a "Life Boat Drill" that was a mandatory exercise. With a bit of trouble, they found their assigned lifeboat station. Marylou carried Bobby in her arms. As it was a rule that everyone had to be out of the cabin and find their lifeboat wearing their lifejackets. There was a small jacket provided for Bobby. No exceptions! They had the Ship's Surgeon's nice big cabin with two anchored bunk beds. Bobby slept in his bassinette, which was tied to a permanent bed leg.

They had taken their sea sick pills [Dramamine] before boarding which really helped when they hit the ocean swells after passing under the Golden Gate Bridge into the Pacific Ocean. They attended a movie that first night. This trip seemed like a real Honeymoon which they never had the time for when they were first married.

The ocean seemed huge, beautiful, and a bit frightening. Neither one of them had spent any time on an ocean. Bobby turned three months old while at sea on the breast of the broad blue Pacific. The water was a deep azure blue as far as the eye could see.

Because they were taking their pills, the rocking of the boat did not bother them. There was some rocking motions even with the ship's stabilizers in use. They would be aboard about three weeks and would land in Japan on August 5th. Bobbie was still taking a night feeding; Roger solved the bottle heating needs by obtaining one from the hospital refrigerator before heading to bed. By leaving the bottle out, it spontaneously warmed to room temperature by the time for his feeding. This procedure worked well until they reached the tropics when the milk would quickly turn sour; so it had to left in the sick bay area until needed. Bobby had to adjust to cool milk which didn't seem to bother him one iota. While Roger was busy with his duties, Marylou and Bobby walked the decks while their cabin was being cleaned and beds made. What a luxury!

The meals were excellent except for the constant supply of only black olives which appeared with every meal, morning, noon, and night. The ship was provisioned every other voyage, they were on the second round; so the green olives were very prominent in absentia. It was a long time after they were back in the States before Roger could look a black olive in the face. Ugh!

Roger explored his medical "Sick Bay" and found out that it contained a well equipped surgical operating room including a trained surgical nurse, a staff of three other nurses and four enlisted personnel. A Master Sergeant managed this area and the enlisted aids, but not the nurses. The surgical nurse was a Captain and was in charge of the nursing staff. Roger felt that he had inherited a competent medical staff and a professional work area.

He had to inspect the food preparation galley each day, hold a troop "Sick Call", and another one for any dependents requiring medical assistance. The rest of the time, he was free to ply his own desires. While they were at sea, Roger received a promotion to Captaincy. He could not purchase any "Captain Bars" for his uniform while aboard ship, but he signed his orders, memos, and other communications as Captain King. This activity really irritated a passenger Lt. Colonel, who was a stickler for Army Regulations [AR's]; however, Roger didn't give a hoot about the irritating Colonel's thoughts.

The passenger Colonel kept trying to pull rank with Roger to obtain special treatment for his companion paramour and came to Roger's cabin one night about 10:00 pm wanting some trivial service for her. Roger told him "NO and to bring her to the Dependent Sick call in the morning". He quietly shut the door in the Colonel's face and went to bed. Marylou was very worried because of Roger's boldness.

His authoritative remarks insulted the Colonel no end. Roger consulted his Master Sergeant who found just the AR which would fit the bill and that would silence the obnoxious officer. The Colonel was given the ultimatum, "Cease and Desist his activities while aboard ship or be put ashore at the next port of call". The Troop Commander approved of Roger's actions. The pain–in-the-tail officer kept his mouth quiet for the rest of the voyage. Marylou was aghast, but Roger was very complacent with the whole affair. He gave, "Many thanks", to his Sergeant. Their voyage continued onward without any more interruptions.

His main duty was inspecting the kitchen [galley] as to sanitation and food preparation safety. When he entered this area, he was appalled and filled with utter dismay. The sanitation for the food preparation was zilch regarding safety features. There were about two thousand troops aboard and nearly seven hundred dependents. A food poisoning outbreak would wreck havoc. The worker bees were foreign contract workers with very little regard or insight for the importance of sanitary food handling.

He immediately demanded that the officer in charge report to him where he read him the riot act and really dressed him down. White coats and rubber/plastic gloves would be worn during all food preparation activities without exception. Hereafter, Roger conducted a "White Glove" inspection every day. Woe to any violations of his orders. Roger's name was "MUD" for the rest of the voyage by any of the workers in the kitchen – officers included. 'So be it', he thought. "There is no way that we will have to cope with an epidemic aboard this vessel".

The first Port of call, where they arrived, was Honolulu in the Hawaiian Islands. An old classmate, Eddie Jones, was stationed at Army Trippler General Hospital doing Internal Medicine. He and his wife, Marge met them at the dock with the typical island greeting of wreaths of flowered leis, which they put around Roger's and Marylou's necks.

They had a small version for Bobby. The Army Band was playing "Far Away Places with Strange Sounding Names" as they came into port and while the passengers disembarked.

It was just happenstance that the Joneses were celebrating their fifth wedding anniversary. Roger and Marylou had attended their wedding on Margie's farm when they were interns. They stayed ashore with the Joneses, who showed them all around the Island of Oahu. They went up over the Pali Pass, where the winds blew constantly in almost in hurricane force; the Punch Bowl where Ernie Pyle was buried; he was a famous World War II wartime reporter. They had a solemn trip to Pearl Harbor which had been devastated by the Japanese in the sneak arrack on the United States on December 11th, 1943. This attack initiated the War with Japan. Roger remembered vividly where he was when he heard the news of the attack. He and his dear friends, Glenn Gustafson and Don Erickson were at Glenn's house getting ready for a picnic. Gus, subsequently, was a fighter pilot and was lost over the English Channel.

The Kings had to be aboard early the next day by 8:00 am. This vessel proceeded out to sea as the band played "Harbor Lights" with the destination of Guam as the next port of call. While at sea and when Roger was attending to any "Sick Call for Troops or Civilian Patients", Marylou was enjoying the fresh air with little Bobby. When Roger was done seeing people, he strolled the decks until he found them. Together, they would slowly amble along enjoying the sea breezes.

The ship traveled on and over the endless expanse of ocean waters. They would spend some time standing at the bow of the ship watching the waves dancing from the bow which was sharply cutting through the water, flying fish were jumping from one wave to another. Similarly, they would enjoy watching from the stern of the boat the magnificent wake, eddying back and forth, which was generated by the two powerful propellers which sped the ship on its forward path. It was an awesome sight seeing the immense wake generated by the propellers.. While strolling the deck, Roger liked to watch the sunrays dance across Marylou's freckled and slightly turned up nose.

After all of the guff and nonsense that they had encountered enroute to this point, Roger was so smitten with Marylou and how she handled their discomforts that it was very apparent to some passengers, who observed them, that he was a died–in-the-wool romantic.

On the way to Guam, they passed Wake Island[11], the "Pacific Alamo", where four hundred marines held off an invading overwhelming number of Japanese forces for ten days, giving the States time too rally to defend our coast line. The Vessel saluted the Island which was just a strip of sand, as they passed by.

They passed the International Date Line where they set the clock back six hours. The crew put on a show as they crossed the line with King Neptune and his supporting cast. It was an entertaining time with the officer class receiving egg shampoos, and eggshells, along with catsup and flour in the face. The initiation included old spaghetti in the mouth.

There was a Man-over-Board Drill where crew members rescued a dummy from the water via a life boat. It was quite an experience watching them launch the retrieval boat and obtain the body. It was an amazing practical lesson in how long it took to stop and turn this large vessel around.

---

[11] Battle of Wake Island Wikipedia

On the way to Guam, the vessel encountered part of a typhoon which shimmied and did a fierce destructive tango with Island of Okinawa, but it wasn't willing to remain stationery where it was. The storm was in constant motion. The ocean was on a fierce rampage as they neared Guam. The sky was as dark as midnight with no stars to be seen. It rained buckets of water; the winds howled like angry banshee demons. My Oh My! How this great vessel was tossed about by the fierce winds and angry, mountainous waves. It was as though this big ship was just a wood chip or cork floating on the top of a boiling cauldron. Looking out their port hole, they gazed in awe at the competing forces of the wind and waves.

There was not a hot meal served for three days. The ship rolled from side to side at the whims of the terrific demonic winds and the angry destructive waves. It was very frightening to the uninitiated. The Island of Okinawa had been in the main path of the storm; it had received the brunt of the storm's force; docks and other installations had been destroyed or severely damaged.

Roger had one casualty from the storm. A seven year old boy was thrown off his top bunk and sustained a simple fracture of his forearm. Roger ordered an x-ray which showed the two ends of the bone in close apposition to each other. He skillfully reduced the break, applied a plaster cast, all the while thanking Dr. Bach, his fellow Orthopedic Resident at the Omaha Med Center, for his expert training. The patient was watched closely for any circulation problems – fortunately, there were none. The various countless rigid army rules, customs, and attitudes were beginning to wear on both Roger and Marylou.

The ocean waves splash against the sides of the vessel and port holes producing a musical serenade of songs of love and devotion that Roger had for Marylou. The storm's breath was fast and eager for a period of time before spinning away and moving on out to sea leaving much destruction here and there.

Roger worshiped Marylou's eyes, lips, laughter, and hands. Whenever he touched her, he could feel her tremble. She was in ecstasy whenever his hands slowly moved over the silky feel of her skin and her exciting and graceful feminine curves. He had come to know her body as well as his own, and loved every inch of it. He felt starlight on her skin and moon dust on her lips. As they stood on the Lido Deck one night looking at the moon, Roger said to Marylou with a breathless whisper in her ears, "We don't just have the moon, we have all of the stars combined with it. Their hearts were totally in synchrony. Ah Love! Sweet Love!

He was always so glad to get back into Marylou's comforting arms at the end of the day; they were the harborage of his life to come. At times he wanted her with a burning hunger which was only calmed by the taste of her kisses. With his fingers in her hair, he would plunder her lips time and time again like there was no tomorrow. They, both, would lose themselves in the throes of their passion. Marylou wanted the burn of his mouth and the scorch of his touch. She felt very safe in his loving arms.

Young Bobby was undaunted by the force of the Typhoon. His bassinette was tied to an anchored bunk, and he seemed to enjoy the rocking of the boat as though he was in a cradle. The next morning, the winds and huge waves had subsided and were gone; the ocean was placid; Guam was beautiful and peaceful as seen from afar. There were many navy ships in the harbor.

As the vessel docked, the army band was greeting the passengers by playing the usual song of "Far Away Places with Strange Sounding Names". The husbands of the passengers swarmed aboard, and the greeting of the families was so touching. Many cried for their joy. It was such a happy occasion. Many families had been apart for well over a year. Marylou and Roger counted their blessings at being able to travel together.

Roger and Marylou did not go ashore on Guam as there was not much to see. They were told that there was all types of surplus army material scattered throughout the jungle, which was available for the picking. What a waste of taxpayer monies!

They picked up about two hundred Engineer Troops from Guam to take to Okinawa to help repair the damages which had been created by the storm. The ship sailed the next day. Once again, they had to turn the clock back as they proceeded towards Manila. There was a dance that night aboard ship with an orchestra made up of the troops that were aboard.

Roger and Marylou celebrated their marriage of three years and seven months. They certainly were an old married couple by now.

Oh! How they loved to dance. They were a sight to gaze upon. They seemed to just glide smoothly around the floor. There was no arm pumping or body jumping jack activities. Their backs were straight, and Marylou's head was nestled against Roger's shoulder and neck where she would whisper sweet nothings in his ear while they danced to the rhythm of the music. They almost seemed as one person as they danced so closely with one another. They enjoyed many different dance steps and were skilled in them; such as the fox trot, ballroom danceing, waltzes, polkas, swing, boogie, and the various South American dances like the rumba – my how Marylou's hips did sway, the samba, The Cha Cha Cha, and several others. People would stop, sit down, have a drink, just to watch them dance as they were so graceful in their movements. The days passed slowly as there was not much going on except walking the decks and watching the waves. There were bingo games and movies but these became boring after awhile.

Manila came. The single typhoon casualty was transferred to the big General Army Hospital for follow up care. Roger was pleased to be removed from any further responsibilities regarding this child.

The Port Surgeon suggested that they borrow his jeep and driver to see the city. There were a large number of sunken Japanese ships in the harbor from the "Battle of the Philippine Seas". Apparently, our forces caught them unawares as they did to us at Pearl Harbor.

As they drove through the bombed out town, the sights were devastating and depressing. Buildings stood like great empty grey ghosts. Half clothed, hungry urchins roamed the streets. People lived like rats in a hovel using parts of a devastated building for shelter with only corrugated sheets for the walls of their dwelling. The people were dirty and emaciated looking. The population seemed to be making almost no effort to better themselves; there was no frantic rebuilding occurring; the people seemed to be rather indolent and apathetic.

There was one water spigot in the center of a street corner for the people to use for obtaining water for a radius of a three block area. To see this mess was to appreciate what destruction had been missed back in the States during the War. The sights were heart rending, and the people seemed so resigned and depressed without making any real strides to rectify their situations. The people's state of mind rubbed off on Roger and Marylou and it had been a very disturbing day.

There was a party that night at the Port Officer's club. They danced the night away, and enjoying champagne until midnight before going back to their ship. For entertainment, they had a wonderful treat watching a tall graceful couple doing Spanish numbers. They moved beautifully and so instep with one another; they moved as one unit and were steeped in each other; they seemed to be oblivious to their surroundings.

They set sail, later, at 10:00 am. The ship seemed almost empty as so many passengers had disembarked to stay at the various stops along the way except for the troops for Okinawa. The ship passed many islands including Leyte[12] enroute to the island. Leyte was so prominent during World War II and was where General MacArthur landed on his return to the Philippines.

Some dependents boarded the vessel to go home to the States with other folks destined for Japan. While aboard, some household tasks were necessary. Marylou did a hand laundry in their cabin each day, which was hung on lines strung by Roger.

Meanwhile, aboard ship, there was the musical murmur of the waves splashing against the ship's hull while softly singing the siren song of the mermaids, who had lured sailors to ply the endless seas from time immemorial. These songs lulled them asleep as they voyaged onward towards their new destiny.

In Roger's mind, there repeatedly echoed the refrain, "What will we encounter, and will I be able to take good care of my family and keep them safe in this new and strange land". Marylou had the patience of a saint and possessed the knack of making a person feel as though he/she was the only person in the world when she was listening to them talk.

They docked at a small make-shift pier in Okinawa as the main dock had been destroyed by the typhoon. Naturally, the band played the usual tunes that they had heard so many times coming into and exiting ports. The troops from Guam were disembarked. Roger and Marylou decided not to go ashore as they were told the Island was not secure and a side arm was necessary to carry when venturing off the ship. Thank you but NO Thanks!

Okinawa was the last stop before Japan. As usual, the ship left about 8:00 am. They arrived in Yokohama about 11:00 am the next day. The harbor was very busy. They saw freighters, steamers, and cruise ships from around the world everywhere they looked. It was an awesome sight. There were large buildings everywhere they looked just like being in the States. A Harbor Master Boarding Party came on the ship with orders for the debarking passengers. Roger was given his orders. They were to proceed to Sendai, which was a town about two hundred miles north of Tokyo.

They were conveyed to the railroad station by an old, rickety bus which bumped along rattling and banging on its way. The train was an ugly relic of an bygone era with very narrow berths to accommodate the smaller Japanese bodies. Marylou and Bobby were in the lower berth. He was just above them. Neither Roger nor Marylou slept much as the train rattled noisily on and on to their next big adventure.

They arrived in Sendai with no one to welcome them. Roger saw an ambulance and commandeered it to take them to the 172nd Station Hospital. No one knew that they were coming. How nice! What a greeting.

---

12 Battle of Leyte Wikipedia

PART 6

SENDAI, JAPAN

THE 172ND STATION HOSPITAL

CHAPTER 20

LIFE IN SENDAI,[13] JAPAN

They arrived at the hospital exhausted, both physically and mentally. The Chief Nurse was kind enough to let them rest in her room. They awoke hearing a constant clicky clack outside the window. Upon looking, they saw a parade of Japanese folks walking on their way to work. They were wearing some type of wooden shoes with small wooden risers holding them off the pavement. It was quite a sight. They learned that in wet weather the risers were higher. The folks wore a white tabby type of foot covering with a split toe to help hold the shoe on the foot.

After he washed and shaved, Roger reported near 11:00 am to the Adjutant of the Hospital. As before Roger inquired about housing, they found out they were to stay in the Guest House in the Kawachi Dependent Quarters area until housing became available, which usually took some time. Ugh!

In the Guest House, they had two large rooms with plenty of fresh air via sliding windows. The faithful hot plate was pressed into service once again for Bobby's formula. Bobby seemed to be thriving on all of the activity. Because of all of the disruptive changes he had undergone, his eating and sleeping patterns left a lot to be desired.

This area was very nice with many trees and expanses of manicured green grass reminding them of Brown's Mills. The many dependent houses were very modern looking making it seem as though they were in the States instead of being in a far off foreign land.

They would strive to make the best of their situation. The Guest Mess Hall was about three blocks away where they ate their three meals. A Guest House worker looked after Bobby when they went for meals.

While Roger was at the hospital one fine day, Mrs. Naimark, the Commanding Officer's wife, came to visit Marylou and Bobby. She initiated Marylou to the Commissary where Marylou bought a few food items and became acquainted with the store where she would be buying her groceries. She quickly became friends with the butcher, who fell victim to her big beautiful brown eyes and gave her great choices of meats. She had learned very early in her life how to use her eyes in order to obtain what she wanted. Roger was no exception to her guiles. To her, Roger's love was quiet and unhurried much like floating in a canoe on a lake with the ripples flowing far and wide to distant shores as the canoe floated lazily along..

The vegetables in the Commissary were grown on a hydroponic farm so they would be safe to eat. Everyone was constantly cautioned not to eat any fruits and/or

---

[13] Sendai, Japan Wikipedia

vegetables from the Japanese markets, no matter how enticing they looked, because of the probability of obtaining parasitic infections. The meat was imported from the States as was the dehydrated powdered milk, which was reconstituted in Sendai. The Army endeavored to keep its personnel healthy and active at all times.

At the Guest House, Japanese girls did their laundry and kept the rooms neat and clean. Life wasn't too bad, just inconvenient. They longed to be in their own quarters and away from prying eyes. They longed for privacy.

In a very few days after the Colonel's wife's visit, Roger was informed that they now had housing. She obviously told her husband that she wanted housing for Marylou and their child pronto! They quickly moved into their quarters in the Kawachi Dependent Area where they had desired to be. Their housing was a duplex, which was completely furnished with all of the necessities for housekeeping including a house girl, Takayama, who worked sixty hours per week at their convenience.

Their quarters included dishes, cooking utensils, a toaster, iron, ironing board, table lamps, a high chair, crib, a play pen, beds, and all the other essential furnishings needed in a home with a child. Because the climate was damp, they were cautioned not to burn a light bulb in the closet continuously due to the danger of a fire hazard. The shipment of Nutramigen arrived shortly after moving into their quarters

The crib was becoming a major necessity as Bobby was outgrowing his bassinette. It couldn't have come at a more useful time. Wow! What a way to live, and what a major convenience everything seemed to be.

They learned that if they wanted to hire another house girl it would be at the rate of six dollars per month. Thank you, but no thanks! Post War Occupied Japan was a very impoverished nation. The people were literally living from hand to mouth. Money was almost nonexistent. The US currency was a prized commodity. There was a very active "Black Market" which did not interest Roger.

The lawns in the dependent area were a dark green and meticulously manicured. There were beds of sassy, colorful flowers around their unit waving a major welcome to their new home.

The Japanese loved little children and called Bobby, 'Babysan". Marylou was "Mamasan" and Roger, "Papasan". Marylou sensed that this coming year was going to be a very special one. She just knew that she felt very safe and secure whenever she was in Roger's loving arms. She was so enthralled when his fingers combed through her hair like they were moving through clouds of misty black strands, and her eyes were the color of a rich chocolate brown. She had such a clear Celtic porcelain type of complexion that she was a delightful sight to gaze upon. With her by his side, Roger was in seventh heaven and ready to conquer the world.

Whenever he could, Roger plundered her lips time and time again until they ignited into a fiery passion for each other. His kisses had her sinking into a soft blue haze. She constantly thought, "I am loved, and I am wanted". This feeling became her secret mantra. She loved him with her whole being of heart and soul.

Oh Joy! His kisses would start feelings beginning with her lips, journeying through her abdomen, and spreading with a tingle clear through her finger tips and toes. She felt that she was in heaven whenever she was in his arms. She could lose herself in his kisses. To know that he wanted her so much was exciting in itself and to know the feeling that she was cherished was a glory for her to have and to hold closely locked in her heart.

Roger spent the mornings at the hospital, had lunch there; then, he was transported via ambulance to his dependent dispensary in the Kawachi area. Here, he saw any dependent patients until all were seen; then he went home, which was just a short stroll from the dispensary to his house.

Sometimes he would come home very early as there had been only a few patients to be seen.; They would go for a walk hand in hand. They explored the area around Kawachi and began to venture further away into the city proper. They walked past the huge Commanding General's house. It was impressive. There were guards stationed by the gate. Takayama watched Bobby while they were away.

They could see feverish rebuilding that seemed to be going on in all parts of the city. Their housegirl told them that Sendai had been devastated by firebombs. The fires were so hot that the population ran to the river to escape the heat. This action worked well until the waters became too hot to endure, and they had to get out. The only surviving buildings were made of cement block. The 172nd Hospital was one of the few survivors and had been an insurance building.

Houses were built to withstand mild to moderate earthquakes. The walls were fashioned out of a mud, sand, and rice straw mixture. This was poured into wooden frames and allowed to harden into a very solid mass. It was a very practical way to build in this earthquake prone land. The floors were covered with woven straw mats. The walls were of a sliding paper material in nature; were colorfully decorated; and could easily be opened or shut to change the dimensions of a room.

Rice was critical to the Japanese economy. Not only was it the main food staple along with fish, but was made into flour for baking – cookies and cakes, fermented into Saki as a wine, and the straw was woven into mats for their houses and beds. Straw was made into large hats and coats for the farmers to use in the fields and was used in building houses. It was an all purpose utilitarian product item of major economic impact. Very little of anything was wasted by the Japanese. By necessity, they were very frugal people.

Roger and Marylou were lying in bed one morning when they felt the bed shake and pictures on the wall were seen to sway. This action was of a momentary nature. Wow! They had just experienced their first quake. With time, they became so use to them that the quakes didn't faze them anymore. They were becoming acclimated to an entirely different world and culture. By being located in Sendai, they saw much more of rural Japan than those folks stationed in the big cities like, Tokyo.

Happily, Takayama looked after and spoiled Bobby while they were out walking. Marylou bought a stroller at the Army PX [Post Exchange] and would take Bobby for walks in the mornings. They led a rather carefree existence. As Bobby grew older, he would rather run than walk. This situation became a game with him. He learned how to sneak out of the stroller when least expected and would run licky-split as fast as his little legs would take him, making Marylou chase him. He would laugh and laugh when she caught him. They had such fun with each other. He could slide down the duplex stairs quicker than one could say, "Jack Robinson". He was a very agile child and as fast as lightening.

It wasn't long until Roger was confronted with a major medical problem at the hospital. The obstetrician notified him that he was about to do a C-section on an rH negative mother with an affected rH positive infant. The severity of the infant was not known, but deemed very bad. Roger scrounged for the necessary equipment from here and there as this was a first for the hospital; no one had any experience except Roger. There was no time to ship the mother to Tokyo to the big army hospital where the necessary expertise was readily available. Roger was filled with many anxieties, doubts, and apprehensions. He sweat profusely while gowning and scrubbing for the surgery.

Jack P. performed the C-Section and delivered a boy, who was already deeply stained with a yellow color in the vernix covering the him. He handed the infant to Roger. This finding was bad news. The infant had to be exchanged pronto. There was no time for dilly dallying on what was needed to done.

Harking back to his days with Dr G., Roger was as well prepared for this event as possible. In lieu of fifty cc's that had been suggested with the case with Dr. Gedgoud back at the med center, he decided to exchange 10 cc's of blood in and out of the infant based upon the autopsy findings and the size of an infant's heart. The exchange continued until he used up an entire unit of O negative blood.

The infant handled the exchange very well. Roger had the previously designated and, the soon to be trained, pediatric nurse monitor the infant's heart rate while he pushed blood in and out of the infant. When the exchange was completed and stabilized, the infant was transferred to the Tokyo Army General Hospital for further care. This move made Roger very grateful to be able to share these immense responsibilities with others.

In the hospital, he was considered somewhat of a hero even though he had only been on this post just a few weeks. Using the smaller amounts of blood taught Roger a big lesson in the physiology of an infant's circulation, which experience he carried with him for ever more.

It had became very obvious early on that there was no trained and/or skilled pediatric nurse on the hospital staff; so he proceeded to train this one who had evidenced some interest in this area and had monitored the exchange. Roger made her his right hand person and proceeded to acquaint her with the differences between pediatric nursing versus adult care. Col. Naimark, the Hospital Commander, readily approved this training. Carol, the selected nurse, thoroughly enjoyed being trained as Roger was such a patient and excellent teacher. These skills added to the admiration that the staff was beginning to have towards him as having an aura of being a very competent pediatrician and a friendly sort of person. Col. Naimark thanked his lucky stars that Roger had been assigned to his hospital staff.

When he wasn't busy with pediatric patients, he had a ward of about sixty men to supervise. These patients had Infectious Mononucleosis, Viral Pneumonia, or Hepatitis. If there were any infectious diseases admitted to the hospital, they would fall under his province. Roger was kept fairly busy all morning; then, after lunch, the ambulance took him to the dependent dispensary in Kawachi. He was very content with his lot as it was beginning to unfold.

At times, he had to take Medical Officer of the Day Duty [OD] and stay at the hospital all night. Marylou felt very safe and comfortable with him being gone as contrasted when he was at Governour's Island or Fort Dix. When he was OD, most of the time there was not much to do. He delivered a few babies and checked some soldiers for sobriety tests; but, mostly it was being there just in case.

One night about 2:00 am he received a call, which he promptly answered. The weak female voice on the line asked him what she could do for her cat with diarrhea. He almost told her what she could do; but recanted just in the nick of time. He was too polite to express what he really wanted to say to her.

One fine day that fall when everything seemed peaceful and quiet all hell broke loose. A child from Camp Schimmelphening was admitted with what seemed to be polio. Help! Oh what to do? He had never seen a case, and neither had anyone else on the medical staff. He quickly went to the scanty hospital library and checked any and all information available, which was very sparse.

The nurse, he had been training, had a smidgeon of knowledge of how an iron lung operated. Roger had no experience, nor had anyone else on the hospital staff; so into the fray he plunged learning as he went. Subsequently, there were fifteen affected children from this same dependent area. Most of them had a lower limb weakness. Panic spread like wild fire throughout the entire army personnel in Japan. At that time, there was no polio vaccine or methods of treatment. Roger felt like he was, "Under the gun" and sitting on top of a spiraling vortex of major trouble.

Fortunately, all the patients recovered seemingly without any residual paralysis. Experts had been flown over from the States to study the why's and wherefore's of this catastrophe. Their collective consensus seemed to be that the polio virus had been water-borne. More sanitary procedures were instituted in this dependent area, and no further cases appeared.

Roger breathed a big sigh of relief when the epidemic subsided. Life gradually resumed a normalcy. His worry lull lasted just a few weeks; his peace and quiet was broken when he admitted a case of Meningococcus Meningitis to the hospital. It was a Major's child. This situation created some serious friction when the Major insisted that he have free access to visit his child. Roger got his back up when he explained and re-explained that was not possible due to the highly contagious nature of this disease. Until the child was into the recovery stages, he would do as Roger instructed. He told the Major to go stand in a corner as he was in charge of his child, and he would not jeopardize the child or the possible chance of starting an epidemic. Col. Naimark backed Roger one hundred percent. End of story!

The child finally recovered to everyone's relief – especially Roger's. Roger's attitude towards some officers was not conducive to a comfortable relationship. A few of the bachelors started to "Come On" to Marylou. He let them know in no uncertain terms that she was "Off Limits"! Enough said.

The hospital planned an outing to a resort area on Matsushima Bay[14], which was a beautiful and a characteristic scenic spot, which could be found on postcards of scenic Japan. A contingent left the hospital in a happy and lively mood anticipating new sights and ocean sounds. They journeyed by bus to this area.

Great fun, an enjoyable picnic, and pleasant time was being had by everyone until tragedy struck. A Japanese hospital worker was caught in a vicious undertow in the ocean and drowned. His body was recovered, but resuscitation was impossible. It was a very solemn and subdued group who were filled with their own thoughts and contemplations, as to the frailty of life, as they returned to the hospital. Everyone became very cogent of how fragile and unpredictable life really was.

---

[14] Matsushima Bay Wikipedia

Marylou and Roger gradually became acquainted with the different officers and their wives who were on the hospital staff. They began to enjoy the company of a homespun couple, Captain Tom and Erma Burnett from Oklahoma. They were raised and schooled in Arkansas. He graduated from the University of Arkansas, Medical School in Little Rock, Arkansas.

The Burnets owned a used jeep and invited Roger and Marylou to go on many rides and have picnics in the countryside. It was fall, and "Rice Harvest" time. As they drove along, they noticed an "Elder Mamasan" rolling grain of rice off the stalks onto a woven straw mat. She had an infant in some kind of shawl carrier on her back while she blissfully worked at shedding the rice grains.

Just a short trip further along the road, a farmer was using a flail to separate the grains of rice. In another area, a man was holding a small metal crank separator to capture the rice. This separator was as modern as it got. Oh my! To separate the rice grains from the chaff, the rice grains were piled on a matt and poured onto another matt on the ground with the wind blowing the chaff away enroute.

The four of them could look and observe rural life as it had been and still the same as it was from several hundred years before. They would have missed these experiences if they had been stationed in the Tokyo or another large urban area.

They realized just how important that rice was to the Japanese culture and livelihood. Rice was, obviously, the main Japanese staple of life. This importance was exemplified by the "Fall Rice Harvest Festival". It was such a colorful situation with the ladies dressed in their best, colorful Kimonos[15] and fancy embroidered Obi's[16] [Sash] around their waist.

Children enacted the story of the season with dancing to the reedy tunes of the pipes, clashing cymbals, and pounding drums. Of course, there had to be a large colorful dragon as part of the story. The festival was quite a show to witness. It was a true "Oriental Event" with all of the trimmings. Roger took innumerable pictures to document this occasion. It was "One of a Kind" occurrence.

There was a Catholic Nursery and a Baptist Nursery in Sendai. On occasion, the Japanese attending physician would throw up his hands over a sick child and say to the Superior, "Call the American Doctor". Most of the cases were those of severe diarrhea and dehydration. The child needed IV fluids which Roger handled easily and with great success. His pediatric nurse would accompany him and soon learned the technique of giving IV fluids to a child.

One day, Roger was called to the Col. Naimark's Office. He found himself on the proverbial hot water and undesirable red carpet for treating the Orphanage children. There was an "All Command" edict about "No fraternizing with the Japanese people". He had to cease and desist or else!

"Well', said Roger to himself, "There is more than one way to skin a cat. Nothing was said about my nurse not going there, she is very capable; so she can go to the Orphanage as my delegate; tell me what she finds; and I will tell her what to do. Any port in a storm will suffice, and the children will be responsibly cared for". This action worked well for the rest of the time Roger was in Japan. As far as he knew, no one was any the wiser and he was obeying the edict. One more irritating Army Red Tape Hurdle was conquered.

---

[15] Japanese Kimonos Wikipedia

[16] Japanese Obi Wikipedia

The daily hospital routine went on seemingly endlessly until the Hospital arranged for another outing. This time, it was to visit a Leprosarium, which was close by in an isolated part of the countryside. There was a busload going, and wives were included. Being a Nurse, Marylou was keenly interested in going on this particular excursion.

The group was briefed while riding to the destination. There were about five hundred patients with about fifty severely affected ones. Previously, they had been told not to wear open toed shoes. Upon arrival, they found out why. They were required to dip their shoes in an antiseptic solution upon entering or leaving any building.

Most of the patients had the skin form of leprosy and had disfiguring lumpy lesions on their external body parts. The fifty seriously affected patients were housed in a separate unit. These patients were frequently blind and/or had lost some fingers, toes, or part of their noses. It was rather a gruesome sight to say the least.

The attending doctor had a beautiful daughter, who was destined to live in this sanitarium for life without the hope of marriage or of having a family. She was ostracized and segregated from the real world.

They learned that when a patient discovered that he/she had contracted leprosy in the southern part the Honshu Island they would walk several hundred miles north to the Sendai Sanitarium and check in as a patient. This action avoided their family being ostracized from society and the real world. Imagine walking that far! Municipal transportation would be denied them. It was a very sober group who returned to the hospital with everyone counting their blessings. This experience made the Bible Stories much more realistic to all concerned.

Back home in Kawachi in a moment of profound thankfulness, Roger pulled Marylou into his arms and whispered softly in her ears with a melodious cooing voice, "I want to give you the sun, moon, and stars"; then, he thoroughly rained kisses all over her. While he was whispering and kissing her, she thought to herself, "I already have the sun, moon, and stars by having you". Stars whirled around within her head along with many loving thoughts. She was a very contented and satisfied lady.

Thanksgiving was approaching; they received a call from Yokohama from Dorothy Brown inviting them to spend the holidays with them. As Roger had this time free, they immediately made plans to take the day train to Tokyo. As they walked off the train, they observed that the Japanese passengers had to join a special line where they were dusted with a DDT powder for lice and ticks. How gross!

They were met by their hosts, the Brown's, who had their own car which had been shipped over from the States. It was present when they arrived in Japan. Such a convenience this was. The Browns had a real Japanese house in town near the hospital, in Yokohama. Johnny was doing anesthesia at the large Army hospital. He had been the first resident in anesthesia at the med center.

They occupied their guest room. When they had unpacked, Bobby met their child, Ann Elizabeth, whom he proceeded to frequently annoy and bedevil her by pulling her hair whenever he could. My, how she squealed! No admonishment to Bobby seemed to have any effect much to Marylou's dimay.

The children were looked after by their housegirl while Roger and Marylou were given a tour of Tokyo; seeing the impressive Emperor's palace, which was surrounded by a moat; the grounds were beautiful to behold. They saw the Dai Ichi Building, which housed the new Japanese Parliament.

The emperor was no longer seen as a God, but was just a figurehead. General MacArthur was able to manage this transition from ancient traditions without any pain or major repercussions from the Japanese people. He had accomplished a miracle in managing the transition of Japan from a feudal nation into a modern society while still preserving their traditions and ceremonies within the space of just a few short years.

They were treated to a trip to Kamakura[17] where the Great Buddha Statue sat in residence. The grounds were immaculate and very picturesque consistent with being on a picture postcard. The Statue had survived since 1252 AD including enduring many severe earthquakes and typhoons. This trip was a sheer delight.

They waited in vain to see General MacArthur leave his Command Offices, which was said to be quite a ceremonial exit. After waiting for a long time, they gave up and left for Yokohama and supper. Roger, Marylou, and Bobby took the day train home on Sunday. They had had a wonderful time over these holidays.

Bobby woke up during the first night home, sick as a dog, with nausea, vomiting, and diarrhea. The next few days were a nightmare. Roger's worst fears had come true. Bobby was very ill, and he, alone, had to care for him; there was no one else available with any pediatric knowledge. Roger carried him day and night until he thought his arms were about to fall off. He tried many remedies to control the vomiting without any relief. As a last resort and before taking him to the hospital for IV's, he tried an old, old fashion home remedy – luke warm coke with a teaspoonful, every fifteen minutes. Thank heavens, it worked! Recovery came fast on its heels, and the household once again resumed normalcy. Marylou quickly vetoed any thoughts of further travel with Bobby. "Once is enough", she said.

Roger learned that there was one of the ten Imperial Medical Schools in Japan in Sendai. He asked Col. Naimark if he would arrange for him to make pediatric rounds there every other Tuesday afternoon. This request was accomplished without any hesitation. Roger learned that the Dean of the school was a Doctor Sato, who was a famous Hematologist [Blood] He had developed a special stain to differentiate the various white blood cells which were circulating in the blood stream and which mainly fought infections and other body states. Roger was able to utilize some of Dr. Sato's concepts when he was back in the States.

The Japanese Pediatric Ward was so different from the States. When a child was admitted, the family moved in with the child to provide the food, blankets, and nursing care. They brought in a small Hibachi on which to cook the food. On the ward, there was a Stateside Diet Kitchen set up for teaching purposes, but was much too expensive for regular use. Hospital care was very primitive to an outsider.

Roger made rounds there every other Tuesday afternoon after his Dependent Dispensary was completed. He encountered some very strange medical situations. He saw a child having many convulsions. In the workup, the skull x-rays showed a calcified ascaris worm in the brain tissue. "How did this happen?", thought Roger. He had gone back to the States before he knew what was the outcome of the worm. The convulsions were controlled by medications.

On another occasion, he saw a child with Nephrosis [a protein-losing state through impaired kidneys]. The child's abdomen would accumulate vast quantities of fluid which

---

17 Kamakura, Japan Wikipedia

would interfere with the movement of the diaphragm resulting in trouble breathing. Shades of Roger's internship and residency with a patient. With Roger's own eyes and when the ascitic fluid was drained off, spun with a centrifuge, and examined under the microscope, unbelievably, all forms of the tick were seen ranging from the larvae, nymph stage, to the adult form of ticks were found. The Japanese doctors were still trying different approaches to eradicate the ticks when Roger left Japan.

He learned that the Japanese medical library was so limited in medical journals due to the War that the access was limited to the heads on the various medical departments. The War had wrecked havoc with more than just the ordinary population, in addition, everything else had been devastated. Dr. Sato requested that Roger see several children in the hospital. He did and gave him his opinion about them. This request was the beginning of Roger's long career in consultative pediatrics, though he didn't know it at this particular time.

With Japanese respect and with politeness, Roger asked Dr. Sato to see a couple of puzzling children with a strange type of anemia [low red blood corpuscles] where Roger learned about Dr. Sato's unique Hemogram where the different white blood cells were reported in actual numbers instead of percentages. This change made a lot of sense to Roger; he carried these concepts with him into his future.

He and Marylou still continued their practice of reviewing their day's activities while preparing supper. It was the nicest part of their day.

One morning, Roger was paged at the hospital, on the phone was a panicky young army doctor with only a nine month internship, on the Island of Hokkaido, which was just north of Honshu. He had a child with acute Meningococcus Meningitis, who was much too ill to evacuate. The young doctor desperately needed help and guidance. After Roger calmed his hysteria down, listened to the child's history, asked a few pertinent questions, and proceeded to outline a plan of treatment for him.

He stressed the importance of a strict isolation technique so that the disease would not spread. He cautioned about the need to control the child's temperature with cold body packs and antipyretics [aspirin]. He calculated the doses of Sulfanilamide and penicillin needed for the specific treatment of the child. The need for IV Fluids was stressed. Last but not least, the parents needed to pray like never before. The doctor was to call him several times a day and report how the patient was doing. Little did Roger know, this experience was another step in the molding of him into a future fine pediatric consultant.

The child gradually improved and was returned to the arms of his parents with his mind and body intact. There were no residual complications. The doctor could not thank Roger enough for his guidance and assistance. Col. Naimark was more than impressed and pleased with his young pediatrician's acumen and reserved demeanor.

Marylou and Roger enjoyed walking through the downtown area of Sendai. They would stop and browse in the many different mom and pop shops. The Mamasan would keep herself busy sweeping the dirt floor of the shop. It was immaculate. The shops were poorly heated; only by a small hibachi. The winters were chilly with a damp coldness to the days that seemed to penetrate to one's bones.

They purchased several different souvenirs such as the Seven Japanese God ceramic figures and other typical native items. They had so much enjoyment looking and visiting with the proprietors of the different shops. These were such carefree days much like being on a protracted honeymoon.

Whenever Roger kissed her, her needs were similar to a jumping off place for her. Roger's name came like a sigh from her lips. They were so in love with love and with each other that to outsiders it might seem to be nauseating.

In Roger's mind, Marylou was certainly the moonlight and roses type. She loved to sing to herself even if it was a bit off key, to him it sounded like the tinkling of a hundred fairy bells. Whenever she would murmur his name in his ear, his heart would pound; he was left breathless.

One of the most treasured thoughts he had about Marylou was, "She was like the taste of a robust vintage wine and created the desire for a bigger and longer sip". Thoughts of her were so powerful that her mere presence could fog up his mind with lyrical memories concerning her and make his imagination soar to the heavens and back again. He always thought of her as his fairy princess as the mere touch of her hands was like magic. He never knew that love could be such a potent force, and how wonderful it could be.

Marylou was never anything like a pushover. She definitely had a mind of her own and enjoyed pondering on an item for awhile before committing herself to a decision. Little did people realize that with all of the adventures that they had endured, love was the glue creating the adhesive force that tied each other so closely together.

As winter receded, the days grew warmer and sunnier. They would encounter groups of school children on excursions with their teachers. The children were all dressed alike in their school uniforms. The boys wore black pants and white shirts; the girls wore dark skirts and white blouses. They were very well behaved.

Nosy Roger asked the teachers all kinds of questions about the school and the curriculums. He learned that the girls starting in kindergarten began learning all about homemaking items and artistic subjects, like sewing and flower arranging, which would be carried throughout their entire years of schooling. The boys would start with math and science early on and continue with these subjects into the foreseeable future. All of the children had to learn Japanese, English, and German throughout their entire school years.

The Japanese cameras and electronics were beginning to give the German industry a run for its money in quality and ingenuity. The Nikon and Canon cameras were to compete successfully with the German Leica Camera for the elite photographic market worldwide. Electronics were beginning to become a major force in corollary industries.

Before he had left the states, Roger had applied to several noted schools in order to finish his last year of training. He received notice that Duke Medical School where a Dr. Davidson, who wrote the book, "The Complete Pediatrician", was the chairman of the department, had accepted him with a stipend of fifty dollars per month. One came from Harvard where there was a place in the outpatient pediatric department with NO Stipend attached. He would have to find other sources for an income. "No thank you", thought Roger to both of these positions. He finally heard from his first choice which was the Henry Ford Hospital in Detroit where his mentor Dr. Tompkins had trained. It paid a hundred dollars per month. Oh Joy! He quickly accepted the position of Chief Resident. He sent regrets to the others.

He had taken a trip to the Mayo Clinic before leaving the States but was not interested in training there after the visit. He had visited several other places prior to his leaving for Japan and had forgotten about them due to his many hospital activities and work load.

Roger harkened back to his time at Fort Dix and his cohort, Elmer Mueller, who currently was in an Internal Medical Residency at Ford. He wrote about finding living quarters. Elmer proved to be real friend by finding and renting an apartment starting July 1 for him. It was just across the street from the Hospital's Emergency Room.

With his immediate future settled, Roger and Marylou settled back and enjoyed the rest of their time in Japan. They took many walks all around the area. They visited the Export Bazaar in downtown Sendai where there was all kinds of Japanese goods. They bought two sets of the noted Noritake China, which were very expensive in the States, but ultra reasonable in Japan. They bought cloth for dresses and suits. The Japanese were accomplished seamstresses and tailors. They were determined to enjoy the days that they had left during their stay.

As the Japanese tailors could make anything one might desire from only a picture, they bought enough cloth at the Export Bazaar for twin Glenn plaid suits and some silk cloth for several cocktail dresses and suits for Marylou. Roger had a tux made as he knew that he would need one eventually. His Mother obtained and sent a tux kit with the satin for lapels and along the trousers and stiffening for to be placed in the lapels. Just for a pittance, these clothes were tailored to fit to a tee.

Spring had arrived and with it came the thousands of beautiful cherry trees in full bloom and were noticeable everywhere one looked. The landscape was smothered everywhere with the lovely pink blossoms. It was that time of the year for the various communities to hold their "Cherry Blossom Festivals. This happening was the biggest customary ceremony of the seasons.

The costumes [Kimonos and Obi's] were outstanding, colorful, ornate and festive. The oriental reedy music set the stage for the many children's songs which told a delightful folk story. Once again, there was the proverbial fiery dragon which caused the girls to squeal and had the boys trying to look brave as they quaked in their shoes. It was special time. Roger took many pictures with his Kodak Retina II camera which he had purchased at the Army PX Store.

On their way home with Tom and Erma, they commented on the zeal and zest of all the building that was taking place in Sendai as contrasted to the intense apathy they saw in the Philippines. The farmers were, especially, eager beaver workers. They would carry buckets of dirt up the nearby hills, find a crevice, and fill it so they could plant some food to grow. The economy was pathetic. The Japanese practiced advanced contour farming which was ages old as contrasted to the States. The hillsides were terraced so the rains, which were plentiful, could irrigate all the growing plants as the water wended itself down the hillside. These contour practices were just beginning to obtain a foothold in the States; whereas, they had existed here for centuries.

Time was quickly passing; soon they would be on their way to Detroit where Roger would finish his formal pediatric training. He only needed one more year because his army service time counted for a year in the pediatric certification requirements. He entertained the thought that he might take two years instead of the necessary remaining one as he was considering an academic life.

He spent much time contemplating his past experiences while in the service. He discussed them at length with Marylou, who had a practical, keen, and sharp mind and also her nursing background

He outlined to her the various areas where he felt that he was lacking in knowledge and experience and those areas where he was strong. He knew what he wanted to accomplish while he was at the Henry Ford Hospital. He was going to discuss the possibility of handling both the Chief Resident's duties and also handling a first year resident's ward for the needed inpatient experience that he was seeking. He was very serious about his future training desires.

He felt very comfortable about his future as they prepared to leave their happy little feathered nest in Sendai and go home. When they received their orders to depart, the army packed all of their belongings and shipped them directly to Omaha where they were put in storage awaiting the end of their time in Detroit.

They left Sendai with blue skies and an air of the new adventure just ahead. They took the day train to Tokyo where their friends, the Browns, met them. They stayed with them for a few days until their boat, the SS Sergeant Freeman, would sail. They would be going home on the "Great Circle Route" past the Aleutian Islands to Seattle; and so it came to pass. The Browns were to follow them in about ten days.

PART 7
ON THE HIGH SEAS AGAIN

CHAPTER 21

STATESIDE BOUND

As they boarded their vessel, it was raining pitchforks. It was hard to see across to the pier to where the Browns stood crowded under an umbrella waving good- bye. There was a saying in Japan, "That if you see Mount Fuji on your way out, you will return to Japan someday". Both Marylou and Roger were sad that it was impossible to see the Mountain. They never returned

Going home on this old rust bucket was nothing compared to their pleasant cruise to Japan. Marylou was housed in a cabin with six other wives and their children. It was a bedlam at best. Roger was stowed in a cabin with four officers one of which was a Dr. Ray Mellinger, who was going to the Ford hospital for an Internal Medical Residency. Later on in life when Roger was in private practice, their acquaintance would be professionally renewed.

Bobby had passed his second birthday while in Sendai and was notably very fast on his feet. He loved to escape his parent's grasp and run helter skelter laughing all the while at playing his game. His parents knew from past experiences, that if they wanted to walk comfortably on the decks, they would have to obtain a harness for Bobby to keep him corralled; and so they did. They were very cognizant of the fact that if he were to wrench loose, he would slip through the ship's scuppers and on into the sea within the wink of an eye.

As they strolled the decks, the wind in conjunction with the waves slapped against the ship's hull singing the song of "Home Sweet Home". The first few day the skies were heavy looking and a dull grey. The atmosphere was fogged with a cold, wispy, mist while the waves sang their endless refrains of the seas. Some days aboard ship were long and weary and would have been boring if they hadn't had each other.

There always seemed to be a flock of sea gulls hovering around the ship's stern waiting for a handout from the dumped garbage the kitchen threw overboard each morning; or they would endeavor to catch some of the mullets which were tossed up by the ship's wake. Their antics supplied a nice diversion from the mundane activities of the day. The waves created from the bow wake were formed into stiff white caps. The gulls constantly looked for tidbits being thrown up by these waves. Roger relished the fact that he did not have any responsibilities for the first time in a long, long time.

At such times, Marylou would dream a montage of images concerning her past life so far with Roger and pondered what adventures they would be encountering in their future time in Detroit. Roger never ceased to thrill her just by looking at him. Sometimes, when she looked at him she felt as though a hornet's nest had taken up living in her stomach. She would feel as nervous as a teenager on prom night.

Roger felt a wonderful sense of wellbeing when her loving hand would slide into his. The magic would make itself felt. It was much better than having a good night's sleep or a well cooked meal. It was such a satisfied feeling that he knew would be carried within himself forever with Marylou was by his side. He never imagined such happiness and contentment could ever happen to him. He so missed holding her in his arms while they slept. He was in love measured somewhere between ecstasy and delirium and all of the points in between.

Some evenings as they stood and watched the waves, Roger would say to her, "We don't need the moon as we have over a million stars watching over us". When he kissed her, she could feel the heat of the sun or the softness of the moon light on her skin even as the evening breezes cooled it. The next early morning's tang of the sea breeze was like a tonic to one's soul. The skies had cleared at long last.

The ocean was a deep, deep blue and very quiet just before dawn, the sky and its horizon was filled with pink streaks and was in complete serenity with itself. It was the best part of their day. When he kissed her while watching the sun break forth, she could feel the smoldering embers from the preceding evening's embraces burst into flames. She was a fortunate lady. They enjoyed breathing in the salt laden air while they walked the decks hand in hand.

This moldy old vessel was one of those ships that Henry Kaiser had welded together in great haste and mass produced to carry supplies and troops to the European Theatre during World War II. They were a major factor in the US being able to out produce and out supply the Nazis Forces. This massive outpouring of all types of supplies led directly to the defeat of Germany.

This poor excuse for a cruise ship had been converted from hauling freight and was put into service for transporting dependents from one place to another. Of any amenities aboard, forget it! They were very few and far between.

There were no convenient through passageways for going from one area to another horizontally between decks. One had to climb the stairs, go to the next compartment, and go down those stairways to achieve one's goal of getting from here to there. Obviously, these ships were not made for convenient traveling but for expediency.

One day when the passengers awakened, they had sailed into a dense fog bank. Their hand could hardly be seen when held close to their faces. The dense quietude and stillness was creepy. The major sound heard was the mournful fog horn of the ship sounding at regular intervals, much like the timed beat of a bass drum keeping a strict tempo for an orchestra. As the fog began to thin, residual tendrils could be seen wrapping themselves around the smoke funnels like banners announcing that they were coming home.

They would walk each day with Bobby in his harness. They were so glad they had it as he was such a lively boy. It would have been almost impossible to keep him checked and in tow. Roger was becoming aware of what a wonderful Mother Marylou was. He loved the way she handled Bobby both when he was nice and when he was being an obnoxious brat; filled with pouts and saying, "NO NO"! She was the type of woman who asked for little for herself, but would give of herself endlessly. Roger would give her the world if it were possible as she asked for next to nothing for herself.

Because they had to live in separate cabins, they greatly missed holding each other in their arms while sleeping; consequently neither of them slept very well. They felt like teenagers when they would steal kisses in one of the ship's corners if they didn't want an audience watching. Marylou was a very private person and didn't like public exposure. When they would walk the decks during the late evening, cymbals would clash in the air whenever they came together in a passionate embrace.

Shafts of the moonlight glow danced, and shimmered around Marylou whenever they came together. The fire of their love would blaze clear and bright as they held each other. It was as though there was no tomorrow or even a yesterday. Time would seem as nothing, and their world stood still. At these moments, she would softly whisper in his ear that she loved him beyond sanity while exuding a soft sweet breathless contentment which was left in its whispered wake. Roger's fingers slowly caressed her face and hair as his would slowly roam through the silky strands of her hair. Roger was gone beyond his own comprehension. He would murmur in her ear that his dreams had already come true.

At times like these, she would tremble when Roger held her close. She had a major set of new feelings every time he held her close to his body. She thought to herself, "Love is a glorious state". Their quiet words and gentle sighs made her skin damp with passion; and, as Roger saw the trust she exuded, he was greatly humbled that he would be able to measure up to her expectations.

As they neared the Aleutian Islands, the weather turned very damp and cold. It was a penetrating type of cold that went right through their clothing while walking on the decks; no matter how warmly they had bundled up.

They passed the Attu and Kiska Islands which the Japanese had occupied during the War, but could not advance any further onto American soil. They were conquered again by the United States after a short interval of their occupation.

Seal Island was passed with seemingly a thousand creatures barking their welcome home. They passed by fringes of Alaska as they journeyed through the "Inside Passage"[18] on the way to the State of Washington. They were on the last leg on their voyage to the States. They landed at Bremerhaven and disembarked with a great sigh of relief to have their feet on good old American soil.

Roger looked at "Old Glory" with its red, blue, and white colors flapping saucily in the wind and heartfelt feelings of pride of being an American burned in his cheat. He saluted for the last time while being in uniform before discharge to return to civilian life. When he made his goodbye salutation to "Old Glory", he choked up and had tears in his eyes as he said, "So long" to the Service. His time had been well spent, and he was a better doctor for it.

It was with a great astonishment with the speed with which they were discharged from the service. It seemed as though they were on their way home to Omaha within the wink of an eye.

Again, during the trip home, Roger had been spending some time, once again, in deep thought about what he needed to learn during his last year of formal training. He knew where he was proficient and what his deficiencies were. He wanted to bolster these weak points while at the Ford Hospital; so he made plans to discuss these needs and ideas with Dr. Johnston when he arrived.

---

[18] Inside Passage Wikipedia

PART 8
BACK HOME AT LAST

CHAPTER 22

OMAHA – "HOW SWEET IT IS"

They flew from Seattle to Denver by United Airlines where they changed planes for Omaha. They had make-shift living quarters while staying with Marylou's Mother's after their return. While in Omaha, Roger visited with Drs Gedgoud and Tompkins. The doctors hinted that if he came back to Omaha there would be a place for him in their practice. This was heady news for Roger and was far beyond his own expectations or dreams that he would be able to practice with his two major mentors. He had so greatly admired them while in training at the Omaha Med Center. In all his travels, he had never seen their like and to practice with them would be a dream come true.

At night while asleep, Marylou's hair was a midnight of silk spread out over her pillow. Roger loved to look at her sleeping, and he would think to himself wonderful thoughts and remind himself, "She is all mine, all mine. How lucky can one man be". At night pressed against him, she felt his warmth and his very being seemed to ooze into her's due to his controlled passion for her.

* * * * *

Roger had some time available before moving on to Detroit. He decided to visit Dr. Henske while in Omaha. The meeting was cordial, but not too friendly as though Roger would be future competition for him.. While there, Dr. Henske asked him what he thought about the North Korean invasion into South Korea. Roger was speechless. Before he had left Japan there had been a rumor that there would be a war somewhere in the Far East, but no one put any credence in the rumor.

The first thought that came to his mind was, "Will I be called back as I was just discharged?" He journeyed home filled with misgivings and anxieties. "Would he or wouldn't he be returned to the service?" was a constant refrain singing through his mind on his way home. He didn't want to worry Marylou so nothing was said. As each day passed, and he didn't hear from the War Department, his anxiety level dropped just a teeny tiny bit more.

* * * * *

It was great to be home in Omaha. Little had Marylou realized or dreamed about how much they would travel and see so many different sights before she left Omaha. She had never been out of Nebraska before her marriage to Roger. Now, in retrospect, she recalled that she had traveled far and wide from the Atlantic to the Pacific Ocean; from Canadian border to the Gulf of Mexico; and, last but not least, seemingly to the far ends of the earth, to the Far East and Japan in only three short years. Amazing!

DETROIT, MICHIGAN

CHAPTER 23

THE HENRY FORD HOSPITAL

Roger relished the fact that he did not have any responsibilities for the first time in a long, long time. After being home a short while, Roger needed to proceed onward to Detroit and start the completion of his training for his pediatric career post haste as July was rapidly approaching. He flew to Detroit; spent a day with Dr. Johnston, who was the head of the Pediatric Department and was noted throughout pediatric circles as an astute physician and a leader in calcium and protein metabolism in adolescents. He was a slender man with a very kindly face and an amusing twinkle in his eye.

Roger reviewed with Dr. Johnson the experiences he had had while in the army, especially, those while in Japan and expressed his desire to handle both the Chief Resident's job and those of a First Year Resident on the Wards as he needed to fill in the several medical areas where he was weak. He was very cognizant of his deficiencies. His goal sought to bolster these weaknesses. Roger had had much outpatient work ad infinatum while in the army. Outpatient work was one of the main duties of the Chief Resident. Dr, Johnson quickly agreed to his plan to forego any of these duties; suggested that he take a few days to become acquainted with Detroit, his apartment, and any other necessities; so he did.

He stayed with the Mueller's – his friend from Fort Dix – for two nights while he checked out his new quarters and started to prepare the apartment at 1215 West Bethune Street for his precious family. He wanted to make it semi-livable for them as soon as possible so that they could be a family once again.

This apartment was conveniently located just across the street from the beautiful hospital grounds and close to the Emergency Room. This location was ideal when he had to be "On Call" at night.

The apartment had a fairly large living room, which converted to the bedroom, when a Murphy Bed stored in a closet was pulled out and down into a useful bed at night; then, was folded and stored away during the daytime. There was a small kitchenette and an enclosed porch where Bobby would have his own room. There was no heat in this room which posed a bit of a problem in the cooler weather. This discrepancy was solved by clothing Bobby in two "Bunny Suits with feet in them so they wouldn't have to worry if he became uncovered during the night. The apartment was not the Taj Mahal[19], but it was going to be home sweet home for the next year.

Roger watched the mails every day like a hawk expecting to receive a service recall notice, but none came. He learned that his Hospital Unit [172nd Station Hospital] was

---

[19] Taj Mahal Wikipedia

the first medical contingent into the fray on the Pusan Peninsula. He felt for his former comrades, especially, the Burnett's. He learned that his intern friend, John Brown, was retained in Yokohama for another year and would remain in Yokohama. He and his family were to come ten days after Marylou and Roger, "Such is life" Roger continued to count his blessings.

Roger's first order of business was to locate and visit the nearest Chevrolet Dealer, which he did. He bargained with the salesman as cars were expected to become scarce again with the Korean War occurring. He settled for a two door sedan, desired for safety for Bobby, and an automatic transmission for Marylou. He remembered her trials and tribulations with the old Studebaker. Ha!

He paid cash, $1500, for the car. They had forgone travel and buying items and expensive mementoes in Japan to save money for this cause. Marylou was a marvelous skinflint manager of their monies. Obviously, cars were much, much cheaper in those long ago and far away days. Roger would take any color available as he was in an urgent situation. The salesman was very accommodating and put a rush order to help Roger.

The next order of business for Roger was to go to the Sears Store where he examined double bed mattresses, ordered one, and, then, to the children's department for a crib, and a highchair. Next, he selected a small kitchen set that would work in that room. Whew! What a job! He was glad to turn over any further purchases to his darling.

An important item on his agenda was making their apartment sweet and clean for his family. He washed down the walls. He thought as he worked, "His family", wasn't that a wonderful sound as he said it aloud time after time. When the phone was installed, he talked with Marylou each night about their different activities.

One night Marylou was all upset and told Roger that Bobby had slipped through the railing at Grandma's open basement steps and landed on the cement floor. She was devastated and crying while telling him. She had taken him to Dr. Gedgoud where he found a broken collarbone. Roger had all kinds of terrifying thoughts flying around in his head as she was taking. A major head injury was the first idea that popped into his mind. When he heard her say, "Broken collar bone", he unconsciously said, "Is that all?" Oh my! The frost that came over the wires would freeze a clay monkey solid. Boy! Was he ever in the proverbial "Dog House". Indignantly, "What do you mean,? "Just what do you mean Is that all?", said Marylou in a most indignant voice. It was a while before he was in her good graces once again.

As he had cleaned and fixed up the apartment as much as he possibly was able, it was time to bring Marylou and Bobby to Detroit. When they talked that night, they made plans to fly there; so they did.

Roger met them at the huge Willow Run Airport. His heart leapt for joy as he watched them disembark. He couldn't have been more excited if it was Christmas. Now they would be a family again.

After getting settled, they took a jaunt to the Sears Store, looked at living room sets and rugs. Marylou decided on a soft green small davenport with a matching chair. They picked out a large dark green shag rug. This was all they could afford at the time. These items were delivered while Roger was at the hospital. Roger concocted a bookcase from glass bricks and 1"x12" three foot wooden planks.

The shag rug proved to be Roger's nemesis after Bobby sprinkled a laundry detergent onto it. Try as he might, only so much could be removed; so when he was up at night,

"On Call", he could feel the grains of the detergent between his toes. Ugh! "Oh that Boy!"

Dr. Johnston made Ward Rounds at 9:00 am whenever he was in town and not out speaking to a medical group. He would relate personal stories to the residents to illustrate a medical point. Having heard the same story several times over, Roger remembered many of them verbatim and used them subsequently in the future when he was teaching students and interns.

It was late July when a severe case of polio was admitted to Roger's floor. He was a big strapping teen, who had been camping in the North Michigan Woods. He was brought in by ambulance. He had bulbar polio, and Roger was introduced to bulbar polio treatment utilizing a hypertonic solution of 50% glucose IV followed by twice concentrated human plasma. The plasma was to retain the fluids in the circulation before being excreted by the kidneys. The goal was to reduce the brain swelling. These IV's were given every four hours. Supportive care was given by a feeding tube into the stomach for nutrition along with oxygen and temperature controlling meds.

All was in vain as this big husky highschool football player expired in spite of all they had done. Other polio patients intermittently arrived at intervals, but most polio victims went to the Herman Kiefer Contagious Hospital. Some of the Ford Residents rotated through this facility, but Roger was exempted from this duty per his request. He had learned all that he wanted and needed to know about polio for future utilization.

Marylou had unconsciously realized this fact but it really hadn't registered in her mind that being married to a pediatrician led to cancelled dates, missed dinners, changed holidays, and interrupted sleep. Other than these few irritants, life with a pediatrician was a wonderful picnic. Ha! She relished the idea that her Roger was really helping people in so many different ways. He not only practiced pediatrics, but he literally lived it. She was so proud of him.

With Bobby, they did not have many precious moments of privacy, but when they did and as Roger held her close, her mind flew elsewhere to a place where dreams come true. At these stolen moments, she knew soon she would have to begin to come back to earth; but for just these few precious moments, she wanted to hang on to her dreams as tightly as possible. When he would kiss her, she would tilt her head so their lips would meet in perfect alignment. She, like Roger, was a pure romantic. They blended together so very well. In less time than it took for a full moon to go from full glory to a mere sliver, love swept over her making her feel swamped with her own emotions.

Marylou made good use of the hospital grounds as a place for Bobby to run and play outdoors. Her major task was to keep him from falling into the fountain and pool as he was fascinated with the large gold fish. One day, he was investigating some bicycles parked nearby, and one fell on him causing a small laceration on the side of his head.

Marylou took him to the ER where the resident put in a couple of stitches. Bobby had just taken off his broken collar bone support. The resident overheard her say to herself, "Will I ever be able to raise this boy in one piece"? The resident smiled to himself. He called Roger; told him what happened; and that he did not need to come as Bobby was more than alright.

One day the phone rang, and the Chevrolet Salesman said that their car was in and ready to go. They were elated. Roger hurried to get the car. He completed all the necessary papers and details; drove home feeling like a king. As he drove, he brought the car near their apartment window, honked; Marylou looked out the window and was elated when she saw a lovely white, two door sedan awaiting her appraisal. It smelt so new. Now, they could explore Detroit at their leisure and convenience; which they proceeded to do forthwith.

They found that the motor traffic was tremendous. Driving in Detroit was nothing like being in Omaha or Philadelphia. It was not labeled the "Motor City" for naught. As they began to drive around, they were introduced to the new and novel "Expressways". These were a Detroit innovation.

Detroit was so big and sprawling that when they wanted to take a drive outside the city, it took them an hour to go from their apartment to the outskirts of the metropolis. They passed the five mile, ten mile, and twenty mile road on the way out and back. These roads circled the city for the convenience of a person getting from one place to another. Exploring Detroit was an inexpensive entertainment and a way to pass their time. They obtained a child car seat for Bobby. He thoroughly enjoyed riding in the car and seldom fussed. When he was tired, he just laid back his little head and went to sleep. He was a great traveler.

One day, Dr. Johnston [everyone called him Johnny – residents included so did Roger after awhile] called him to his office and told him to meet him at the Hospital Garage which was just adjacent to the grounds and gardens near their apartment. Johnny drove out to Dearborn, a suburb where the Greenville Village and the Henry Ford Museum were located. On the way, Johnny related the story of the Museum's conception, and how Henry was afraid that much of the nation's historical heritage was in danger of being lost. He gathered several essential artifacts together and placed them in the form of a village; thus the Village was born.

The Illinois Springfield Courthouse where Lincoln practiced law; Stephen Foster's Home complete with a lake and a good size stern paddle wheel boat plied its way around the lake; the Wright Brother's bicycle shop; the McGuffey one room school where the McGuffey Reader originated for first grade use; the original Ford Auto Factory; and Tom Edison's Menlo Park Laboratory where he invented the electric light bulb were all located there. He even imported stone by stone a Wales Cotswold Cottage. There were many other essential historical artifacts that were part of this Village.

Because Henry felt that the Village was empty and needed children, he established a school so that children could be present running, and shouting. It was a wonderful place to study some of America's History. He wanted the children to live in history.

There was a separate building for all types of agriculture machinery from an early Flail, which they saw used in Japan, to a huge modern field combine. There was another building for just transportation items ranging from a Pharaoh's Chariot to the Ford Trimotor Airplane. The village and Museum were intriguing and marvelous places to spend time exploring many aspects of history. These were magnificent exhibits and was very educational.

Roger's job was to journey to the Village every Monday morning and be the school's physician. The school had children from kindergarten through twelfth grade. He would be giving sex education classes to the highschool teens This was long before any other school did. Help! When he first arrived, he would check with the school nurse and handle any problems that she had encountered during the previous week.

The school let the children live with history in the different buildings that Henry had salvaged and saved from destruction. The Village had all sorts of exciting places to explore for Marylou and Bobby while he was busy doing his assigned tasks. When completed, he would join them. They would walk hand in hand around the place enjoying the sights. Bobby would run ahead of them. When he returned, he would babble like a brook though no one could understand a word he said. His parents were so proud of him.

Roger had to be back on his Ward by 1:00 pm, and so the days quickly sped from one into another as was he so busy

On another occasion, Johnny told Roger to check out a car and driver to Henry Ford II's home on Gross Point Boulevard, check the two daughters, and give them their immunizations for a trip to Europe. Swell! There was a security protocol to be followed when making such a trip to the mansion.

First, he called the front gate phone and described the car and gave the license plate number he would be driving. The mansion was magnificent. The guard at the entrance gate checked Roger and the car to be sure that he was legitimate. This guard rode with Roger up the very long drive to the house where another one met them. The new officer escorted Roger upstairs to where the daughters were located. Roger performed the necessary tasks, and called Johnny about how everything was. With this guard, he retraced his footsteps out of the house. This guard called the gate keeper to finish escorting him off the estate. Wow! What an experience as to how the upper crust lived. Many months later, he had to repeat this process as Caroline, one of the girls, was ill with a cold.

As they explored the city, they visited Cranbrook, the local Art Museum, Colony, and School. Later on, Belle Island, which was located in the middle of the Detroit River, where there was a playground for Bobby to enjoy. They, especially, liked driving along Gross Point Boulevard where the Auto Hierarchy had their big spacious homes. They greatly enjoyed driving out to Orchard Lake area where the sky was so blue, the air so fresh. Their carefree time was so precious.

Over time, their exploring took them up the Michigan side of the Detroit River to Port Huron where they crossed to Canada and came down along the Canadian side to Windsor, which city was just across from Detroit; and, then, back home they went.

As they became acquainted with the other residents and their families, the wives would occasionally get together for coffee. They brought their children. Marylou joined in and brought Bobby. All went well for awhile until one day she came home in total embarrassment. It seemed that two year old Bobby kept bullying a larger five year old boy by chasing him constantly onto his mother's lap. Oh Me! Oh My! It was awhile before she ventured forth with him again. She wondered, "Am I raising a monster"?

Life went along in a quiet seemingly undisturbed fashion with the wives' gatherings until another mighty embarrassing moment occurred. The ladies had collected. Unbeknownst to anyone's mother, one of the children left a large deposit on the floor. All the mothers grabbed their children by the seat of their pants. "Who was the guilty person"? Naturally, Marylou was embarrassed once more. She, momentarily, entertained thoughts of throttling Bobby. Oh the price of motherhood!

Old Henry Ford had another idea that there was something contained in tobacco that was very harmful to people. He commissioned Tom Edison, a very close friend to

Henry, to find out what the ingredient was. Nicotine was found to be the culprit. No one was allowed to smoke in any Ford Building or Factory.

At the hospital, there was a mass exodus at break time during the morning and afternoon periods and again over lunch. The hospital workers were not happy campers about this edict!

Forward thinking, Henry tried to conduct a major social experiment. He reasoned that when farmers couldn't work during the winter that they could be trained to work in his factories and vice versus when the factories were shut down during the summer for retooling, the workers could work on the farm. The experiment quickly went nowhere as the factory workers were not about to become farmers or vice versus; so Henry's great solution to unemployment died a very early death.

Back at the hospital, work on Roger's Ward was moving quietly along. He had developed a knack of being able to draw blood from seemingly impossible veins. He was more adept at this than any of the residents; they frequently called upon him for assistance. One day, Elmer Bastion, having nothing but trouble with a vein, asked Roger to try, which he did. He called from the treatment room across the hall to the resident office where Elmer was sitting and said, "Elm! I was able to get the blood out of your turnip".

As he stepped out of the room, there stood an irate mother who minced no words with Roger for insulting her child by calling him, "A Turnip". Roger learned then and there a huge lesson, "Be careful what you say and where you say it." This lesson lasted all the rest of his life. Talk about embarrassment! No apology would satisfy or be sufficient in this situation to the child's mother's satisfaction.

One day, Johnny called Roger into his office and told him that he was to teach the Ford Junior Nursing Students their semester course of pediatrics. "What next?" he thought, "Shades of Dr. Henske". When he returned home and told Marylou, she congratulated him for the great opportunity and trust. There was no sympathy in her voice; Roger did not obtain any desired solace from her. He pouted awhile until he learned of its futility. "So be it", he thought and got to work on preparing the lessons. His books had arrived from home including his much desired set of "Brenneman's Practice of Pediatrics" reference materials along with other articles which had been shipped from Omaha. Marylou had prepared and decided what items they might need; and so it came to pass. He was rapidly learning the art of multitasking which attribute would be refined and honed many times over the years.

He held the class for an hour each Tuesday morning. He spent many hours and evenings on developing the needed lesson plans for the each class. He had to create tests and grade the papers. These latter tasks were not his favorite chore. Strangely enough, the students liked his teaching methods and gave him a big hand when the course was over.

Johnny had another little task for Roger up his sleeve. He was to go to Wayne State University School of Nursing; teach a course on the newborn infant; which course, was to be followed with another one on the Premature infant. Roger did so with gusto. These classes greatly helped him to understand the delicate body systems in these babies when he had to perform the next Exchange Transfusion.

With a passion, he delved deeply into the physiology of the newborn to better understand the dynamics of these infants. Because of his past experiences, he taught his fellow residents how to conduct an exchange transfusion. He was well liked and respected by them.

On Wednesday mornings at 11:00 am, the residents gathered, including Johnny, and drove to the Detroit Childrens' Hospital where the Chief of Pediatrics, Dr. Paul Worley, held sway. He conducted excellent Clinical Conferences on selected cases. Sometimes, Johnny was asked to add his two cents to the discussion concerning the current case, which he gracefully did.

They went to the same Childrens Hospital on Thursday mornings to listen to a Dr. Wolf Zuelzer, a magnificent pediatric pathologist, who conducted a clinical pathological conference. It just so happened that Roger had been in Sendai with Dr. Zuelzer's Cousin, who was the orthopedist at the 172nd Hospital. Small world!

Roger was rapidly filling up his plate with all kinds of goodies and loved every minute of it. Marylou was so pleased that he was receiving such training and being exposed to so many different ramifications of pediatrics.

When he would come at night, he would gently and firmly gather Marylou into his arms, breath in her intoxicating sense of a woman, and kissed her as if he hadn't seen her for days, and days; finally, he would relax after another hectic day which had been crammed with all sorts of needs and activities.

Marylou gloried in his loving caresses and gave a soft sigh of contentment. "Could life be any better than this"? She thought to herself. In turn, when she wasn't busy, she would let her mind dream thinking about his slow devastating manner which would put butterflies in her stomach. She couldn't resist the dangerous power of the hurricane of love or its rumblings like a volcano about to erupt. These were glorious feelings within her.

* * * * *

Roger heard about a special school based upon a child's developmental milestones. He asked Dr. Johnston about It. He happened to be very cognizant of this school and arranged for Roger to attend the lectures series which were given to the school's patrons and parents during the evening hours. It was the Merrill Palmer School of Child Development.

He listened to talks by obstetricians, psychologists, social workers, and others. It was a very expensive and exclusive school. He began to formulate some more thoughts about his own series of talks when he was in private practice similar to those given by his mentor Dr Tompkins.

While visiting with George Kempton, a fellow resident, he learned that he could do some moonlighting work at a local hospital. Roger asked him the ropes about obtaining a job to supplement his income. He began to work one night a week at the St. Francis Hospital in Hamtramick, Michigan; a city within the confines of Detroit with its own Mayor, police and fire department, and its own school system. At that time, this was a community of over two hundred thousand Polish people, more than any city outside of Warsaw, Poland.

He would work in the Emergency Room one night a week and receive $25 for working from 6:00 pm to 6:00 am. This money certainly made their living considerably better. Marylou did a magnificent job of managing their finances. They no longer had to live from hand to mouth. Against Marylou's wishes, Roger would, once again, donate a unit of blood at periodic intervals as he had done back at the Omaha Med Center. These donations really helped their budget. Because most of the Polish people spoke their native tongue, there was an interpreter in the ER with him. Sometimes, Roger would have to deliver a baby if the attending Polish Doctor could not get there in time or was too lazy to come for the delivery.

One day while shopping at the grocery store, Marylou inadvertently laid her purse down. Right before her eyes, it disappeared never to be seen again. She was devastated as her purse contained all of their funds for the month. Help! In desperation, she called her Mother for a loan of $50, which tided them through until Roger's next paycheck.

Dr. Johnston called Roger to his office and told that he had another interesting task for him. He was to supervise the special adolescent ward where ongoing calcium and nitrogen [protein] balance studies utilizing cortisone were being conducted. Johnny had previously conducted studies on thyroid and several other hormones in a similar manner. These patients lived and went to school in the hospital for an entire year while the studies were being accomplished. It was a state financed study conducted under Johnny's auspices.

All the patients had had a positive skin test for tuberculosis and a healed Ghon Node [calcified TB bacillus] visible on the chest x-ray. Roger's role was to check the girls once per week. All of the girls were on a nutritiou standard diet of 50% carbohydrate, 35% fats, and 15% proteins. On this diet, their calcium and nitrogen elements were in a positive balance [meaning more of these food stuffs stayed within the body than were eliminated]. When the girls began their menses and their period of rapid growth and development began, then, the balance would spontaneously become negative [meaning the body lost more than it stored]. This imbalance would remain negative until after about twenty-seven menstrual cycles had passed; then, the balance would spontaneously return to a positive nature without any shift or change in their diet. The medical significance of this observation had far reaching ramifications. During the negative phase some of the patients would have a spontaneous breaking down of the calcified nodes in the lungs with a resulting reactivation of the tuberculosis. This occurrence required active treatment. These changes could be documented by chest x-rays.

His colleague, Jim Sweeny, a pediatric pathologist resident, did the urine, stool, and blood analysis each week on the patients. Roger learned much about conducting medical investigative studies. He was like a sponge desiring to learn as much as he could possibly absorb.

Roger would go to the x-ray department each week when the Pulmonologists [Lung Specialists] would check the lung status of any active tuberculosis patient in the hospital as to their most recent status. They would decide how much air needed to be instilled into the lung cavity to keep the pneumothorax [collapsed lung] working properly so as to arrest the disease process in the lung and to let it heal. They would, also review the chest x-rays on the adolescent girls, which were taken at periodic intervals.

On another occasion, Johnny gave Roger a number of papers, which he planned to submit for publication. He was to read, check the content, word flow, and determine if the paper described had reached the desired conclusions. Johnny frequently told him that when a paper was deemed completed, "Put it in a drawer, wait a month, take it out, and if it still says what you desire then submit it for publication". Later in life, Roger followed this dictum to the letter.

One day, Dr. Phil Howard, Johnny's right hand man, asked Roger to come to the nursery. He explained that he and Johnny were going to conduct special studies on newborns; they wanted him to check the babies daily for any apparent changes; so he did. Once again, Roger was learning how different clinical investigations were planned and conducted. These techniques were etched in his mind to be resurrected in his future years..

There was an Internal Medicine Resident, Jim Lovelace, who lived near them. His folks had given him a TV, which was quite a luxury in those days. The Lovelace couple invited several of the Ford Residents to come over on Tuesday nights to watch the boxing matches. There was a local Irish welterweight boxer, who was an excellent fighter with many wins. He was fast and shifty. He wore a fight bathrobe with shamrocks on it when going to and from the ring. These figures were, also, on his boxing trunks. He was very light on his feet and could bob, weave, and dance around his opponent like a banshee whirlwind.

The wives brought snacks and soft drinks to enjoy. They would munch on cookies, popcorn, and other items. It was a fun night. These gatherings became a standard social event each Tuesday, and everyone looked forward to the gathering with relish and exchanging gossip. Heaven forbid!

Marylou was an anchoring fixture for Roger's many tasks. These feelings kept him thinking that whatever he was doing was important to their future. He thanked his lucky stars that she had wanted to marry him. His love for her knew no bounds. He was so grateful that she was his helpmate. Sometimes, her kisses demanded all of his strength and all of his energy. She was his lodestone without a doubt. It was wonderfully exhilarating feeling for her to know that he was left reeling frequently by his total and complete love for her.

Everytime he held her hand, magic flowed from her into him with an unrelenting force. In return, his love for her flowed through him like floodwaters after a heavy downpour of rain. He had such pleasurable feelings that cheerful sounds would come to his throat as she kissed him. She found his lips were soft and fitted on her's firmly with warm sensations flooding through her.

Roger arranged with Johnny for his week's vacation to be used in March. They decided to drive home all night hoping that Bobby would sleep most of the way. It was going to be a long and arduous trip. It was seven hundred miles from Detroit to Omaha; and so they went.

They ran into a major snowstorm just outside Des Moines, Iowa. The snowy hills and big semi-trailer trucks behind bothered Roger very much on the down slopes. He, especially, worried what would happen if they might have to stop quickly. Snow was frequently splashed onto the windshield as a truck would pass them which created great problems with visibility. This trip was not a picnic. Roger was relieved when it was completed.

They had a great visit with the family. The meeting with Drs. Tompkins and Gedgoud couldn't have gone better. There would be no "Buy In" to join them. Roger would have a draw of $500 per month with it being amortized by what monies he would put on the books. The arrangements were like receiving a wonderful gift from the "Good Fairy". This step was easily the one to make without any qualms.

As for a place to live, they could rent the first floor apartment next door to the office which the Doctors owned on the same terms. Back to Detroit, they went filled with all kinds of hopes and expectations. On the way, they stopped overnight rather than make the trip all at once, like they had on going to Omaha.

Roger told Johnny of his plans. He was very sorry to lose Roger as he had never had a better resident. Several pediatricians in Detroit made offers to Roger, which were hard to refuse; but he politely declined. Their Shangri-La[20] was in Omaha.

Meanwhile, Roger learned about taking tours through the huge Ford River Rouge Auto Assembly Plant[21]. A new ford was driven off the line every few minutes; so they went to enjoy this outing. The Plant was located in Dearborn, Michigan, a suburb of Detroit.

Before the tour started, they learned that Henry was a genius in the development of the automated assembly line. He was also a control freak on quality of his cars. In order to ensure the quality he desired, Henry owned all of the raw materials that went into any Ford product. The Ford Company owned iron mines in South America and coal mines in West Virginia and all of the other ingredients needed in manufacturing a car.

They watched the process of making glass from essential raw materials, like sand, into polished windows and windshields. They watched them being swung into the appropriate place and installed at the precise moment when needed.

Starting with a basic chassis, the assembly line moved along with different parts being put into place at the appropriate times and places and being fastened into position by a worker on each side of the line. Each worker had an assigned task. Wonders of wonders, they watched a finished car roll off the line and being driven away. Amazing! It was a very enjoyable and informative trip.

They were told that the "Irish Hills" would be an enjoyable short trip to take. The Hills were about fifty miles from Detroit. One day, they took off and drove there. The rolling hill country was pleasant, but nothing spectacular to their eyes; they enjoyed the outing. At long last, early June arrived. The time to go home had come. They packed their belongings and arranged to have them shipped to Omaha. They left Detroit without any qualms; this lack of feelings was much different than when they left Japan.

---

[20] Shangri-La - Wikipedia

[21] Ford River Rouge Plant Wikipedia

EPILOGUE

They bid good-bye to their friends and left Detroit with few regrets. They journeyed home to start the next phase of their life together; so far it had been filled with one adventure after another. New horizons and dreams beckoned loud and clear.

As they drove along and while both Marylou and Bobby were napping, Roger, once again, reviewed his training and preparations for entry into the exciting prospects of practice. He mulled over his unique experiences that most pediatricians never had the opportunity to encounter. He knew that he had shored up his inadequacies and felt confident to handle whatever medical situation that he might encounter.

His mantra became, "Bring it on, I am ready"! So it came to past. Their furnishings arrived just a few days after they did. They moved into the first floor apartment next door to the office. There was a small yard enclosed with a chain linked fence; it was safe place for Bobby to play outside on a busy street.

Roger was welcomed to the office with a mild celebration. He already had some patients booked for him to see. His space was on the north side of the second floor of the duplex. He had an office and a large room which was subsequently divided into two examining rooms.

Marylou helped him decorate with drapes for the windows and wall paper that would appeal to children. He already had his own medical instruments, but, he needed a nice desk set with a blotter and ink stand. Now! He was ready to take on the pediatric world.

His mentors' offices were on the first floor along with the business offices. The basement had been converted into space for two pediatric dentists and an other area was utilized for parent talks. The entire complex was very compact and efficient. It worked well for about ten years when they outgrew this space and decided to move.

Mary and Obie at 68 Years

Curriculum Vitae
Revised and Updated April 2013

BYRON B. OBERST, M.D., F.A.A.P.
(Fellow of the American Academy of Pediatrics)

EDUCATIONAL BACKGROUND

Grade Level Year School Degree Location

1. Elementary: 1937 Saratoga Omaha, Nebraska
2. Secondary: 1940 North High Omaha, Nebraska
3. College: 1944 University of Omaha BA Omaha, Nebraska
4. Graduate: 1946 University of Nebraska, College of Medicine MD Omaha, Nebraska
5. Internship: 1947 University of Nebraska Hospital Omaha, Nebraska
6. Residency: 1948 University of Nebraska Hospital Level 2 Omaha, Nebraska
7. US Army: 1949 Post Pediatrician Fort Dix, N.J.
8. US Army: 1950 172nd Station Hospital Sendai, Japan
9. Residency: 1951 Henry Ford Hospital Detroit, Michigan Level 3
10. Private Practice: 1951-88 Omaha Childrens' Clinic PC Omaha, Nebraska
11. American Board of Pediatrics Certificate #4126 October 26, 1952

MEMBER OF THE FOLLOWING SOCIETIES

1. American Academy of Pediatrics, 1951 to 2013
2. Northwest Pediatric Society, 1951 to 1961
3. ebraska Pediatric Society (including Presidency in 1958) 1951 to 1988
4. Midwest Clinical Society (including Chairman of Section of Pediatrics in 1957), 1951 to 1976
5. Omaha-Douglas County Medical Society, 1951 to 2001
6. Nebraska State Medical Society, 1951 to 2001
7. American Medical Association, 1951 to 2001
8. Nebraska Heart Association, 1951 to 1970
9. Catholic Physician Guild, 1951 to 1960
10. Pan American Medical Society - Pediatric Section, 1965-1983
11. Fellow, Section of American Academy of Pediatrics on Child Development, 1963 to 1987
12. Charter Member of the Society for Adolescent Medicine, 1968 to 1983

13. Fellow of School Health Physicians, 1970 to 1973
14. Fellow, Section on Community Pediatrics, American Academy of Pediatrics, 1972 to 1987
15. Society for Computer Medicine, 1973 to 1982
16. Great Plains Organization for Perinatal Health Care, 1976 to 1977
17. Charter Member of the Sports Safety and Health Care Society, 1977 to 1988
18. Nebraska Chapter, American Academy of Pediatrics, 1951 to 1988
19. Nebraska Chapter Chairmanship, 1976 to 1979)
20. American Association of Medical Systems and Informatics, 1982 to 1990
21. American Association of Mental Deficiency, 1984 to 1986
22. Fellow, Section on Adolescence, American Academy of Pediatrics, 1982 to 1987
23. Fellow, Section on Computers and Other Technology, American Academy of Pediatrics, 1984 to 2010
24. Affiliate, Medical Group Management Association, 1988-1989

ACTIVITIES

1. Instructor in Pediatrics at Wayne University School of Medicine, Detroit, Michigan, 1950-1951
2. Instructor in Pediatrics at Henry Ford Hospital School of Nursing, 1950 - 1951
3. Director of Residency Program University Nebraska College of Medicine and the House Staff at Children's Memorial Hospital, 1951-1954
4. Instructor in Pediatrics at the University of Nebraska College of Medicine, 1951-1954 and 1.1. Associate 1954-1959
5. Instructor in Pediatrics at Creighton College of Medicine, 1951-1954
6. Vice-President of Catholic Physician's Guild, 1959 (Member, 1951 to 1960
7. Instructor in Pediatrics at St. Catherine's School of Nursing, 1952-1955
8. Secretary of Staff of Children's Memorial Hospital, 1952-55
9. Lecturer for Foundation for Understanding, Inc., 1952-1954
10. Assistant Clinician for Heart Diseases for Services for Crippled Children, State of Nebraska, 1953-1960
11. Clinician in Charge of Nursery at Nebraska Methodist Hospital, 1957-1960
12. Member of Infection Control Committee at Nebraska Methodist Hospital, 1957-1960
13. Treasurer of Staff at Children's Memorial Hospital, 1958
14. Assistant Professor of Pediatrics, University of Nebraska College of Medicine, 1959-1969
15. President of Catholic Physician's Guild of Omaha, 1960
16. Director of Adolescent Clinic, University of Nebraska College of Medicine, 1960-1963
17. Pediatrician-in-Charge of Pediatrics and Newborns, Bishop Clarkson Memorial Hospital, 1963-1976
18. Pediatrician-in-Chief, Archbishop Bergan Mercy Hospital, 1965-1966
19. Adjunct Professor, Psychology, Bellevue College, Bellevue, Nebraska, 1966-1968
20. Vice-President, Medical Staff of Children's Memorial Hospital, 1966-1968

21. Director of Adolescent Clinic, Children's Memorial Hospital, Omaha, Nebraska, 1967-1970
22. Chairman of Youth Committee, Nebraska Chapter of American Academy of Pediatrics, 1976-1981
23. Board of Directors, Operation Bridge, Suburban Youth Guide lines: Drug Counseling Service, 1968-1973
24. President, Staff of Children's Memorial Hospital, 1968-1970
25. Associate Professor of Pediatrics, University of Nebraska College of Medicine, 1969-1977
26. A.M.A. Physician's Recognition Award, July 1, 1969, 1973, 1976, 1979, 1983, 1985
27. Nebraska State Medical Association, Committee on Mental Health, 1971
28. Omaha-Douglas County Medical Society, Committee on Education 1971
29. Society for Adolescent Medicine, 1. Member of Committee on Private Practice, 1971-1978; 2. Chairman of Subcommittee on Insurance and Other Third Party Payees, 1976-1978
30. Nebraska Chapter, American Academy of Pediatrics, Chairman, Committee on Medical Practice, 1971-1976
31. Nebraska Chapter, American Academy of Pediatrics, Alternate Chapter Chairman, 1974-1976
32. Member, Committee on Standards, Society for Computer Medicine, 1974-1978
33. Chairman, Committee on Standards, Society for Computer Medicine, 1974-1977
34. Member, Committee on Child and Youth Health Care Standards, American Academy of Pediatrics, 1976-1979
35. Chairman, Nebraska Chapter, American Academy of Pediatrics, 1976-1979
36. Member, Board of Directors, Society for Computer Medicine,1976 to 1977
37. Professor of Clinical Pediatrics, University of Nebraska College of Medicine, 1977 to 1988 when I retired
38. Nebraska State Medical Association, Committee on Medical Ethics, 1977
39. Alternate District Chairman, District VI, American Academy of Pediatrics, 1979-1983
40. Appointment to Committee on Practice and Ambulatory Medicine, American Academy of Pediatrics, 1979-1980
41. Member, Committee on Legislative Issues, American Academy of Pediatrics, October 1979 to July 1980
42. Chairman, Chapter Chairmen's Forum 1. Committee, American Academy of Pediatrics, 1978-1979, 2. Consultant to the Committee, 1980
43. Member, Committee on Medical Education, American Academy of Pediatrics, 1980
44. Chairman, Committee on Standards, Society for Computer Medicine, 1980-1982
45. Member, Credentials Committee, Children's Memorial Hospital, 1981-1984
46. Member, Committee on Scientific Programs, American Academy of Pediatrics, 1981-1982
47. Member, Long-Range Planning Committee, Children's Memorial Hospital, 1981 to 1985
48. Member, Nominating Committee, Children's Memorial Hospital 1981-1984

49. Chairman, Committee on Standards, American Association of Medical Systems and Informatics, 1982-1985
50. Chairman of the Automated Pediatric Special Interest Group, American Association of Medical Systems and Informatics, 1983-1985
51. American Academy of Pediatrics Representative to the AMA Advisory Council for CPT4, 1983-1986
52. Liaison Member for the Omaha Metropolitan Medical Society Executive Committee to the Omaha Douglas County Board of Health, 1982-1984
53. Chairman, Section on Computers and Other Technology, American Academy of Pediatrics 1984 to October 1988
54. Member, Council on Sections, American Academy of Pediatrics, 1985 -1986
55. Member, Physician Advisory Board to Phycom, Fisher-Stevens Co. Physician Communication Network, 1984 to 1986
56. Member, Clinical Diagnostic Scientific Advisory Panel, Clinical Diagnostic, Inc., 1985 to 1987
57. Chairman, Children's Memorial Hospital Computer Committee, 1984-85
58. Chairman, Region VIII Medicine Division of Ombrea Association on Mental Deficiency
59. Member, Clarkson Hospital New Medical Records Committee, 1984-85
60. Member, Clarkson Hospital Medical Record Committee, 1985 to 1987
61. American Academy of Pediatrics Task Force on New Technologies, 1984
62. Senior Consultant, University of Nebraska Medical Center, 1988 to 2010
63. Medical Advisor, Medical Computer Management, Inc, 1988 to 1992
64. Chairman Subcommittee on Practice Management of Retired Physicians for the Metro Omaha Medical Society, 1989-1994
65. Medical Consultant and Advisor, Healthcare Business Solutions, Inc. 1991-1995
66. Medical Director, Omaha Division, Plasma Alliance December 1992-2007

Civic Duties

1. Member of Omaha Exchange Club, 1952-54
2. Guest Lecturer for PTA at many Omaha Schools, Public and Parochial
3. American Academy of Pediatrics Representative to the National PTA Convention in Omaha, 1957
4. Boy Scout Activities:
   1. Public Health Merit Badge Examiner, 1952-60;
   2. Committee Member of Cub Scout Pack at Christ the King School 1957-58;
   3. Committee Member of the Boy Scout Troop at Christ the King School 1959
   4. Scout Master, Troop #370, Christ the King School 1960-1967

5. Guest Lecturer for YMCA Family Retreat Camps
6. Guest Lecturer for many various church young people groups
7. Guest Lecturer for various school teacher groups
8. Founder and Member of Board of Directors, Omaha STAAR Program for School Learning Disabilities, 1968-1978

9. Member, Committee on Health Planning of the Health Planning Council of the Midlands, 1976--1978l
10. Member, Omaha Douglas County Board of Health, 1982 to 1984
11. Immanuel Lakeside Village Community Foundation Committee Member 2012 to Date

PUBLICATIONS

1. Acute Nicotine Poisoning: Case Report, Byron B. Oberst, M.D. and Ross A. McIntyre, M.D., Pediatrics, Vol. II, No. 4, p. 338, April 1953
2. Circulation Time in the Newborn Infant, Using the Fluorescein Dye Method: Byron B. Oberst, M.D., and Fritz LaRoche M.D.: Journal of Pediatrics, Vol. 45, p. 581, 1954
3. Pseudohypoparathyroidism: Report of Case, Byron B. Oberst, M.D., and Charles A. Tompkins, M.D.: AM. J. of Dis. of Children, Vol. 90, No. 2, p. 205, August 1955
4. Congenital Anomalies of the G.I. Tract: Byron B. Oberst, M.D. and Lucy Radicia, M.D.: Nebraska State Med. Jr., February 1955
5. Preventive Care of Infants and Children, IV Influence of "Guided Growth" on Feeding and Sleeping Patterns of Children Clinical Applications, Charles A. Tompkins M.D., Byron B. Oberst M.D., Jeanette Peterson Hamlin B.S., Nebraska State Med Jr., Vol. 38, p 435, December 1953
6. Preventive Care of Infants and Children, V Infant Feeding and Colic: Charles A. Tompkins, M.D., Byron B. Oberst, M.D. and John L. Gedgoud, M.D., Nebraska State Med. Jr., Vol. 40, p. 128, April 1955
7. Paroxysmal Tachycardia with Cerebral Embolis: Case Report: Byron B. Oberst M.D., Journal of Pediatrics Vol. 44p.203-204, February 1954
8. Colorimetric Determination of Blood pH; Willis F. Stanage, M.D., Byron B. Oberst, M.D. and John N. Brown, M.D.: Jr. of Pediatrics, Vol. 47, p. 571-575, November 1955
9. Exchange Transfusion Technique and Use of Aqueous Adrenal Cortical Extract as an Adjunct to Treatment, Byron B. Oberst M.D.: Ne St. Med. Jr., June 1956
10. Chalasia and Achalasis: Children's Memorial Hospital Staff Conference: Byron B. Oberst, M.D., Ralph C. Moore, M.D., Carol R. Angle, M.D.; Nebraska State Med Jr., p. 251, May 1957
11. Participation in Modern Medicine Forum with L. Diamond, W. Zuelzer, Byron B. Oberst, M.D.: Comments on Exchange Transfusion with Packed Red Cells, June 1958
12. Treatment of rH and Related Blood Problems: Clarkson Hospital Staff Bulletin, October 1959, Byron B. Oberst, M.D.
13. Preventive Care of Infants and Children VI: School Adjustment Problems and Their Relationship to "Guided Growth"; The Journal Lancet, July 1966, Vol. 86, p. 331, Byron B. Oberst, M.D.
14. Preventive Care of Infants and Children VII, A Perspective on Adolescence in General, Ne State Med Jr., June- July- October 1969 1969, Byron B. Oberst, M.D.

15. Preventive Care of Infants and Children VIII, Adolescents and Some of Their Social Problems, Including Parenthood: Nebr. State Med. Jr., Byron B. Oberst, M.D., Sept. and Oct. 1970

16. Preventive Care of Infants and Children IX, Unlock the Door on Youth Problems: Nebr. State Med. Jr., July-August 1971, Byron B. Oberst, M.D.

17. Preventive Care of Infants and Children X, An Anticipatory Guidance Program for General Pediatric and Adolescent Office Practice: Clinical Pediatrics November 1971, Byron B. Oberst, M.D.

18. When is a Child Really Ready for School?: Medical Times, June 1972, Byron B. Oberst, M.D.

19. Book: Practical Guidelines for General Pediatric and Adolescent Office Practice: Charles C. Thomas, Publisher, January 1973, Byron Oberst M.D.

20. A Community Approach to Specific School Learning Disabilities: The Omaha STAAR Project: Journal of Learning Disabilities. Aug.-Sept. 1973, Byron B. Oberst, M.D.

21. The Development of Norms and Guidelines for Office and Hospital Medical Care and Clinical Medicine and the Computer: Proceedings of the Fourth Annual Conference of the Society for Computer Medicine, 1974, Byron B. Oberst, M.D

22. A Total Health Care System as Viewed by a Private Practitioner: Part I, A Composite Overview; Pediatrician 4: 176-189, Byron B. Oberst, M.D., 1975

23. A Total Health Care System as Viewed by a Private Practitioner: Part II, A Conceptual Design; Pediatrician, 4:372, Byron B. Oberst, M.D., 1975

24. A Total Health Care System as Viewed by a Private Practitioner: Part III, Progress Report: Pediatrician, 4: 383, Byron B. Oberst, M.D., 1975

25. A Private Practice System Utilizing the Computer and the Problem Oriented Medical Record: Computer Medicine, October 1975, Byron B. Oberst, M.D

26. Current Status of the Language System in Clinical Medicine, Proceedings of the Fifth Annual Conference for Society for Computer Medicine, 1975, Byron B. Oberst, M.D.

27. Language System for Patient Care -- Patient Centered Health System: Proceedings of the Fifth Annual Conference of the Society for Computer Medicine, 1975, Byron B. Oberst, M.D.

28. The Need for a Commonality of Purpose, Design and Application of Computers within the Medical Specialty Organizations, Jr. of Clinical Computing, Vol. 5, No. 2, 1976, Byron B. Oberst, M.D.

29. Society for Computer Medicine, Committee on Standards Progress Report and Workshop: Proceedings of the Sixth Annual Conference of the Society for Computer Medicine, November 1976, Byron B. Oberst, M.D.

30. Common Goals: Working Together: Proceedings of the Sixth Annual Conference for the Society of Computer Medicine, 1976, Byron B. Oberst M.D.

31. Why There is a Need to Determine School Readiness: A Philosophical Discussion Based Upon Long- Term Experiences: Byron B. Oberst, M.D., Pediatrician, 8:133-139, 1979

32. What Constitutes a School Readiness Examination? The Component Parts, Byron B. Oberst M.D., Pediatrician 7: 305-310 ; 1978

33. The Administrative Anatomy of the Pediatric Practice of the Future: Byron B. Oberst, M.D., Pediatrics, 18:1, p. 9-11, January 1979

34. The Parents Guide to Child Raising: Glen Austin, M.D., Julia Stone, Olive and John C. Richards, Spectrum Books, Prentice- Hall, Inc., 1978, Contributing Author. Byron B. Oberst M.D.

35. Book: Computer Applications to Private Practice - A Primer: Co-editor, Byron B. Oberst, M.D.; R. Reid, M.D., April 1984 Springer-Verlag

36. Computers in the Modern Medical Office: Update: Computers in Medicine, November-December 1984, Vol. II: No. 6

37. Guidelines for User Access to Computerized Medical Records, Jelovsek, F.R.; Bolinger, R.E.; Davis, R.E.; Long J.M.; Oberst B.B., Reid, R.A., Zimmer J., Journal of Medical Systems, Vol. II, No. 3, 1978

38. Medical Record Linkage - Panel Discussion; Smith, M.E.; Wendl, H.F.; Jelovsek, F.R.; Oberst, B.B.; Journal of Clinical Computing, Vol. 13, No. 2 & 3, 1984

39. Book: Computer Application to Private Practice: 2nd Edition Oberst BB, Long J., Springer-Verlag, 1988

40. Clinical Benefits of a Life Long Medical Record, Oberst, B.B.; Medical Documentation Update, Institute for Medical Record Economics, Inc., V.6, N.3, August/September 1988

41. Oberst, B.B.; Chapter: Doctor Office Systems: Standalone and Linked; Healthcare Information Management Systems: A Practical Guide; Edited by Marion J. Ball; Judith V. Douglas; James W. Albright; and Robert I O'Desky; Springer-Verlag; 1990

Papers Presented to Various Audiences

1. Northwest Pediatric Society: Exchange Transfusion Technique, Bay Port, Minnesota, 1956

2. Regional Meeting of American College of Surgeons, Omaha, Nebraska, Erythroblastosis and Related Studies, 1957

3. Midwest Clinical Society:
   1. Exchange Transfusion,
   2. Poisoning
   Symposium, 1957

4. Nebraska Heart Association: Congenital Heart Disease, Panel Discussion with Doctor Coburn, 1958

5. Midwest Clinical Society, Resuscitation in the Newborn, November, 1959

6. Midwest Clinical Society, Infections in the Newborn Nursery, November 1961

7. Midwest Clinical Society: Panel Discussion,
   1. What's New in Pediatrics?
   2. School Adjustment Problems and 3. Phenylketonuria,
   November 1962

8. Iowa League of Nurses, Annual Meeting, Adolescence, Spring 1962

9. Iowa League of Nurses, Western Division, Adolescent Motherhood, November 1962

10. Sioux Falls Medical Society, October 1964, Problems in Adolescence

11. Adolescence in General, Sioux Falls, South Dakota, South Dakota Medical Society, March 1966

12. Nebraska Obstetrical Society, Las Vegas, Nevada, Erythroblastosis, New Developments, December 1966

13. District II Nebraska State Teacher's Convention, Omaha, Nebraska, The Trying Years (12-16) of Adolescence, November 1967

14. District II and District VII, OB-GYN Nurses Convention, Adolescents and Their Problems, Including Parenthood, 1967

15. Panel, Member Sex Education in the Schools, Annual Meeting Nebraska Association of School Administrators, November 1967

16. Midwest Section of OB-GYN Society, November 1967, Problems in Adolescence

17. Dodge County Medical Society, Des Moines, Iowa, March 1968, Problems in Adolescence

18. Teacher's Workshop, Fremont, Nebraska, The Trying Years in Adolescence, January 1968

19. The Pediatrician Looks at Adolescence, Omaha Midwest Clinical Society, October 1968

20. Panel on School Learning Disabilities, Omaha Midwest Clinical Society, October 1968

21. Iowa League of Nursing, Symposium on the Adolescent Years, (Early-Middle-Late), October 1969

22. District 9 Teacher's Convention, Kearney, Nebraska, Junior High Section, The Changing Adolescent, October 1969

23. Panel on Counseling the Adolescent, Omaha Midwest Clinical Society, November 1969

24. Round Table on Anticipatory Guidance, American Academy of Pediatrics, Byron B. Oberst, M.D., Co-Leader with Charles A. Tompkins, M.D. of Tucson, Arizona, Annual Meeting, San Francisco. California, October 1970

25. Guest Lecturer, Tri-County Family Practice Postgraduate Course, Denison, Iowa, May 1972:
    1. Continuum of Growth,
    2. Preventive Counseling of Teenagers

26. Guest Lecturer, Fourteenth Annual Seminar for Pharmacists, October1973, Omaha, Nebraska; Discussion of the Role of Medications in the Minimal Brain Dysfunction Syndrome [Attention Deficit Disorder]

27. Panel Member, Omaha Midwest Clinical Society, October 1973, The Pediatrician's Role in Evaluating and Handling Children With Learning Problems

28. Adolescent Nursing Seminar, Children's Memorial Hospital, Omaha, Nebraska, Processes of Growth and Development, April 1973

29. Helpful Guidelines in Understanding Adolescent Behavior, School Nurse Lecture Series, Omaha, Nebraska, May 1974

30. Round Table, Minnesota Chapter AAP, The Relative Value Scale and Its Application, May 1974

31. Panel on Learning Disabilities, Omaha, Nebraska; State Convention Nebraska A.C.L.D., April 1974,

32. Round Table on "Anticipatory Guidance", American Academy of Pediatrics Spring Meeting, Denver, Colorado, April 1974

33. Panel on Recertification, American Academy of Pediatrics Spring Meeting, Denver, Colorado, April 1974

34. Methods of Health Care Audit in Private Practice, Society for Computer Medicine, New Orleans, Louisiana, November 1974

35. A Total Health Care System: Seminar on Health Care Delivery Systems, Sponsored by the University of Miami, Miami, Florida, November 1974

36. Adolescent Masturbation, Nurses' Association, American College of Obstetrics and Gynecology, Nebraska Section, April 29, 1976

37. Patient Education, Committee on Standards, American Academy of October 1976 Pediatrics Workshop, Annual Meeting, Chicago, October 1976

38. Workshop on Medical Records and Related Data, Committee on Standards, Society for Computer Medicine, Annual Meeting Boston, November 1976

39. The Effective Use of Time - Office Management, American Academy of Pediatrics, Course on Continuing Education, Monterey, California December 1976

40. Management Planning and Techniques for Quality Control – Office Management, American Academy of Pediatrics, Course of Continuing Education, Monterey, California, December 1976

41. Cost Accounting, Budgets and Overhead Components – Office Management, American Academy of Pediatrics, Course on Continuing Education, Monterey, California, December 1976

42. Workshop-Office Management, American Academy of Pediatrics. Course on Continuing Education, Monterey, California, 1876

43. Round Table, Minimal Brain Dysfunction, [Attention Deficit Disorder] American Academy of Pediatrics Spring Meeting, New Orleans, Louisiana, April 1977

44. Round Table, Modern Office Practice, Department of Health, Education and Welfare, Institute for Medicaid Management, Orlando, Florida, December 1977

45. Seminar: Practice Management, North Dakota Chapter of the American Academy of Pediatrics, Fargo, North Dakota, April 1978

46. Anticipatory Guidance Program for General Practice, Summer Meeting of the Iowa Association of Family Practitioners Okaboji, Iowa, July 1978

47. Problems in Adolescence, Summer Meeting of the Iowa Assoc. of Family Practitioners, Okaboji, Iowa, June 1978

48. Course of Medical Economics to the Freshman Class of the University of Nebraska College of Medicine in Conjunction with Dr. Roger Mason, Medical Director and Vice-President of Nebraska Blue Mason, Medical Director and Vice-President of Nebraska Blue Cross and Blue Shield, April 1978

49. The Anatomy of a Modern Pediatric Practice Workshop, Society for Computer Medicine, Minneapolis, Minnesota, October 1978

50. Straub Clinic, Honolulu, Hawaii, Modern Pediatric Practice, March 1980

51. Children's Hospital, Honolulu, Hawaii, Practice Management, March 1980

52. Children's Hospital, Denver, Colorado,
    1. Computer Networking,
    2. Computer Applications to Office Practice,
    November 1982

53. University of Southern California, Los Angeles, March 1983,
    1. Postgraduate Course on Computers, Keynote Address: Computers, Computers, Computers;
    2. Computer Applications to Office Practice

54. Workshop on the Handicapped Child Teacher-In-Service Training, Red Oak, Iowa, March 1983

55. Section on Computers, American Academy of Pediatrics, A
    1. Personalized Medical Textbook Utilizing the Computer, Fall Meeting AAP Chicago, September 1984,
    2. Spring Meeting, Atlanta, Georgia April 1985

56. Pediatric Section, American Association Medical System and Informatics Fall Meeting, Washington, D.C., Personalized Medical Textbook Utilizing the Computer, 1985

57. Determination of Wellness-Fitness: Computer Assisted, First National Symposium on Fitness, Las Vegas, February 1985

58. University of Southern California: Third Annual Symposium on Computers, Los Vegas, Nevada, April 1985
    1. Introduction to Accounting
    2. Introduction to Word Processing
    3. Hidden Office Costs
    4. Personal Finances and Other Computer Applications.

59. American Academy of Pediatrics, Continuing Medical Education Course on Computers in Pediatric Medicine Course Coordinator
    1. Computers, Computers
    2. Introduction to Networking
    3. Hidden Office Costs
    4. Personalized Medical Textbook Utilizing Computers
    5. Vendors and Their Problems
    New York City, September 1985

60. Mental Retardation: A Medical Viewpoint, American Association Mental Deficiencies, Region 8, Omaha, Nebraska, October 1984

61. Adolescence: Talk to Junior High Teachers, Fremont, Nebraska August 1984

62. Section on Computers and Other Technology, American Academy of Pediatrics, Computers and Practice Analysis San Antonio, 1986

63. National Conference on Computers, The 8 Management Areas of Office Practice, Chicago, 1987

64. SCAMC Annual Meeting, Tutorial BBO with John Long PhD on Computers in the 4 Office Areas of Health Care Delivery
The 4 Patient Areas of Health Care Delivery, Washington D.C.; 1987
65. Clinical Benefits of a Life Long Medical Record; 4th Annual Meeting of the Institute on Medical Records; New York, April 1988
66. Computers in Private Practice Management, World Med 1988; Minneapolis, Minn.; June 1988
67. The AMOS System and Practice Management, Annual Users Group, MCMI Omaha, Ne June 1988
68. AMOS, Can a System really be that Good?, Iowa Medical Association, Des Moines, September 1988
69. Graphics and Spread Sheets in the Analysis of a Medical Practice; Annual Meeting, American Academy of Pediatrics; Section on Computers and Other Technology; San Francisco, October 1988
70. Computers and the AMOS System in Medical Practice Management; Grand Rounds, Phoenix Children's Hospital November 1988
71. Practice Management Seminar Utilizing the AMOS System Omaha 1989
    1. Phoenix February 1990
    2. Phoenix January 1991

72. The MCMI Marketing Module
Annual AMOS Users Group MCMI
Omaha June 1989
73. Where in AMOS Do You Find?; Annual AMOS Group; MCMI; Omaha, Nebr.; June 1989
74. MCMI Centralized Credentialing System; Iowa Medical Association Services and the Iowa Hospital Association; Des Moines, Iowa; March 1990
75. MCMI Centralized Credentialing System; Milwaukee Medical Society, Milwaukee, Wisconsin; May 1990
76. MCMI Executive Support Services for Physicians and Administrators; Annual MCMI Users Group; Omaha Nebraska; June 1990
77. Practice Management Seminar Utilizing the AMOS System; Phoenix, Arizona; January 1991
78. Management "Beyond Billing": Future Trends in the Automation of Practice Management; Iowa Medical Services, a Division of the Iowa Medical Association; Des Moines, Iowa; June 1991
79. Seminar on AMOS Reports: What Are They and How to Use Them?; Annual MCMI Users Group Meeting; Omaha, Nebraska; June 1991
80. A Computerized Patient Health Record; Iowa Medical Services, a Division of the Iowa Medical Association; Des Moines, Iowa, October 1991
81. Seminar: How to Save Money Through Better Efficiency and Quality Control of the Functions of Your Medical Practice; Omaha, Nebraska; February 1992; Sponsored by Medical Computer Nebraska and Healthcare Business Solutions, Inc.
82. Seminar: The Impact of Living Wills, ADA, and CLIA'88 on the Medical Practice; March 1992; Sponsored by the Lutheran Medical Center of Wheatridge, Colorado and Healthcare Business Solutions Inc.,

83. Seminar: How to Promote (Market) Your Medical Practice; Annual MCMI Users Group Meeting; Omaha, Nebraska; June 1992
84. Seminar: CLIA'88-An Update-- Are You in Compliance?
Sponsored by the Lutheran Medical Center of Wheatridge, Colorado and Healthcare Business Solutions, Inc November 1992

Honors Received

1. Who's Who in America Universities and Colleges, 1943 and 1944
2. Recipient of Honorary Lifetime Membership PTA, 1970
3. Recipient of Honorary Lifetime Membership National Association of Childrens' Learning Disabilities, 1974
4. Recognition Dinner, Children's Memorial Hospital - Twenty- Five Year's Service, November 1976
5. Recognition Dinner, Nebraska Methodist Hospital - Twenty- Five Year's Service, 1976
6. Who's Who in Nebraska 1976-77, Bicentennial Edition, Merit Publishers, Inc., Omaha, Nebraska
7. Who's Who in the Midwest Edition, Marquis, 1978-79, Who's Who's Who Inc., Chicago, Illinois
8. Wyeth Award for Outstanding Small Chapter, American Academy of Pediatrics, October 1977, New York
9. Recognition Dinner, Bishop Clarkson Memorial Hospital - Twenty Five Year's Service
10. Special Recognition Award - American Academy of Pediatrics, District VI Meeting, New York, N.Y., October 24, 1982
11. Men of Achievement, Vol. 10, International Biographical Centre Cambridge, England, 1984
12. Who's Who of Intellectuals, Vol. 6, International Biographical Centre, Cambridge, England, 1985
13. Who's Who In Omaha, 1986 Edition
14. Emeritus: Senior Consultant Status, Department of Pediatrics, University of Nebraska Medical Center, 1988
15. The American Academy of Pediatrics established "The Byron B. Oberst Award" for excellence in computer applications in Pediatrics; 1989
16. The North High School "Vikings of Distinction: Award 2006: "Hall of Fame"
17. Omaha Childrens' Hospital and Medical Center : "Legends in Pediatrics: Award 2006 "Hall of Fame"

Books by B.B. Oberst M.D.

1. Practical Guidance for Pediatric Practice and Adolescent Practice
2. Computer Applications to Private Practice Co-Editor: R. Reid M.D.
3. Computers in Private Practice Management: Co-Author J. Long PhD
4. Reflections on Pediatric Medicine from 1943 to 2010
A Dual Love Story

5. A Tale of a Mother, Her Three Boys, and Their Dog
   The Love Story of a Father for His Family
6. Brownie Bill and the Health Pirates
   A Story of Body Defenses
   Book in Production
7. Miracles and Other Unusual Medical Experiences
   Third Book in this Trilogy
   Manuscript
8. The Golden Years
   Living in a Retirement Center

Printed in the United States
By Bookmasters